VERONIKA VAN DUIN, born in Scotland, trained as a nursery nurse. For many years she lived with people with special needs, together with her own family, and later took in teenage boarders. Her experiences led her to search for ways of creating a home that could contribute to a truly sound and healthy society. In 2000 she published her popular book *Homemaking as a Social Art*. She has recently retired from care work, but continues to run seminars and workshops for homemakers. She is married, has three grown-up children, and enjoys looking after her grandchildren.

Homemaking and Personal Development

Meditative Practice for Homemakers

Veronika van Duin

Sophia Books

Dedicated to all homemakers:
May you find the source of strength you seek.

Sophia Books
Hillside House, The Square
Forest Row, East Sussex RH18 5ES

www.rudolfsteinerpress.com

Published by Sophia Books 2008
An imprint of Rudolf Steiner Press

A catalogue record for this book is available from the British Library

ISBN 978 1 85584 212 0

Cover by Andrew Morgan Design incorporating a photograph by Aliki Sapountzi
Typeset by DP Photosetting, Neath, West Glamorgan
Printed and bound in Great Britain by Cromwell Press Limited, Trowbridge, Wiltshire

Contents

Preface

It is a great responsibility to offer advice of any kind. The meditative exercises I learned and practised for over 40 years, each of which has been a source of strength to me at one time or another, inspired me to offer help to other homemakers struggling with their tasks and responsibilities. I discovered many of these exercises by studying Rudolf Steiner's anthroposophy. Others I learned from various sources, often by word of mouth, and they have become part of my personal practice. It is quite possible, though, that you may find other and better ways of practising them.

When I began to try to practise meditatively, my children were very small and I could not find any time in the day to be alone. I complained bitterly about this to an old friend, who pointed out that I use the bathroom several times a day. He suggested I use it once a day just to meditate. He said it was as good a room as any other, and might serve me until my children were older and more independent.

Though it is not good practice to begin with an apology, I feel obliged to admit that I do not always manage meditative exercises when I should, and often fail to practise them with enough regularity to make them as effective as they can be.

However, this does not invalidate the exercises, nor the real need to work with them. I have benefited, and still do, from my efforts. To keep trying is perhaps more important, and realistic, than to achieve perfection.

I have found that practising the spiritual activity of homemaking brings undeniable rewards: of strength, courage and enthusiasm. I wish my readers much joy in their own endeavours.

I wish to thank Siobhán Porter, Christine Lammers, Fenya Sharkey, Ingelore Maier, Vibeke Alfred, Valerie Wright, Frédérique van Duin, Roxanne Lennard, Turid Engel, Gisela Schlegel, Paula Lindenberg, Korrie Hoffman, Kitty Henderson, Eva Urieli, Marianne Gorge, all of whom gave advice and encouragement.

Prologue

A Prayer

May wisdom shine through me.
May love glow in me.
May strength penetrate me
That in me may arise
A helper of mankind,
A servant of holy things,
Selfless and true.

Anon*

---

* Michael Jones, *Prayers and Graces* (Floris Books, Edinburgh)

Introduction

I began my career as a homemaker 40 years ago. I set out to do what I loved doing with enthusiasm and a great deal of idealism, and looking back I can truthfully say I still love the task. However, if asked whether it was always fun, lovely and free of problems, I would have to say that, though enjoyable, it was never without challenges.

I had absolutely no idea of the magnitude of the task. I knew that I wanted to keep the house lovely, warm and clean. I knew I was going to be responsible for the physical needs of the people at home, and I knew I would be responsible for their health care, as well as their social development. I knew all this because I had a one-year-old daughter and that's what she needed. I also realized that I had become the focus of all these activities and that I found myself very, very wanting indeed. I discovered that no matter how much enthusiasm and love I intended to bring to my task, in reality I felt guilty, pressurized and inadequate much of the time. I became increasingly conscious of my personal short-comings. I also felt very alone, and sometimes lonely too, despite my house companions.

If you're facing a problem you seek advice and assistance from more experienced people. To my amazement I could find little guidance other than the sympathy of fellow homemakers, who rallied round to share their problems. It was a great support to know that I was not the only home-maker struggling with personal challenges; and this started me on a lifelong search which led me to new discoveries about myself and the task itself. In the process I gained insight into principles and processes of life that are active in all of us. I gradually realized that these processes need to be cultivated and harmonized, both inwardly and outwardly. The home-maker sets the tone and ambience within the home, so it follows that she* is required to know herself very well and to address her shortcomings. In my enthusiasm for the task, this realization became an exciting challenge.

Generally, the members of a house community go out about their own business for much of the day whereas the homemaker, especially if she has decided that homemaking is a worthwhile job, stays at home, often alone. There may be small children at home too, or an elderly person, but she can feel as though she has been deserted by her peer group and that she has no one to talk to. So there is nothing to distract her from her thoughts and feelings other than the daily routine, which she may, as I did, secretly feel incompetent to manage. Guilt and insecurity coupled with lack of experi-ence, contrasting with a clear, idealistic aim (which sadly is not sufficiently respected in our modern career-orientated culture) often results in feelings of resentment, self-pity and entrapment. We can forget that we have chosen to be homemakers, and begin to hold it against the others, who are 'so lucky' to get out of the house and away from responsi-bility—even more so if we have not consciously chosen the task but found it thrust upon us due to circumstances.

Of course this gloomy picture does not colour every day of the week or month. But it can creep into small corners of our

---

* I will use the feminine form to denote the homemaker but I am very conscious that increasing numbers of men are taking on the task. It is awkward to write he/she on each occasion. Please therefore include 'he' within 'she', for many male homemakers are doubtless encountering similar issues.

life, sitting there and gnawing at our purpose, even festering into personal resentment towards one or other household member. And because we know, deep down, that the problems are our own personal challenges and should not really be blamed on anyone else, the guilt can start up all over again. A truly vicious circle!

The more I learn about homemaking and homemakers, the more I hear such stories. We expect to cope with a task that challenges us physically, socially and spiritually. And we *are* challenged, not so much by the big things that come towards us, which we can overcome with sound common sense, good management skills, and a large dollop of luck. It is rather, in my experience, the small insignificant events that trip us up. When a child is ill we call the doctor, obtain nursing advice and get on with it. We can even cope with sleepless nights when children are ill, knowing they will get well again and that we will be able to sleep again.

But how can we overcome the irritations that small children create by their sheer energy when we feel tired? In my experience being tired is a fundamental problem. Being cheerful no matter what is another, similar challenge. Any honest homemaker will tell you that cheerfulness really *does* make the world go round—if only it were possible all the time!

And what about producing the delicious meals everyone expects every day? Is it possible to be inspired by the culinary art all the time, every day, for years on end? And then, other people are permitted and even supposed to have life-shattering problems, especially in their teens, but the homemaker should *never* be one of them! She is meant to be always on an even keel, ready to support the poor sufferers around her. Not to mention her partner, who comes home exhausted after a hard day's work and therefore *cannot* be asked to do anything to help. After all, she is at home all day so she has had all that free time, a very common misconception held by other members of the house community.

Now, you may well say that I am being extremely negative. I beg to differ. I believe I am merely describing. Of course, not every day is fraught with disappointment, resentment, guilt and misunderstanding. On many occasions our children's energy energizes us too, and we thoroughly enjoy their creativity and imagination. And when everyone thanks the cook for the inventive and daring new recipe she has put on their plates, she enjoys the knowledge that innovative cooking is really worthwhile. Besides, what can be more touching than a teenager confiding in you, even if it is 4 a.m.? What an honour to be seen as a friend! Moreover, it is such a relief when your partner comes home, sits down with feet up and becomes the quiet focus for a while, giving the homemaker a chance to have five minutes to herself.

It is becoming increasingly acceptable to share the task of homemaking, one partner replacing the other. Without a doubt such an arrangement is very rewarding as long as both homemakers share the same approach and are confident in each other's skills so that each feels free to discuss the issues that arise. Where two people take up the task under one roof, it is perhaps even more essential to explore the following chapters so that real harmony can be sustained.

So what decides why things go well one day and badly another? The events are the same, the homemaker is the same, yet on one occasion nothing works out for her and on another everything seems miraculously to fall into place. Is there a special ingredient in us that we can tap into and cultivate to generate the longed-for equilibrium? This essential question led me to new discoveries, which have proved to be very helpful. They provide basic life tools that can help us in overcoming personal hindrances.

1

Can Meditative Exercises Solve Problems in Daily Life?

Body, life, soul and spirit

The human being is made up of four different elements: mineral, water, air and warmth. The ancient Greeks based their medical approach on this knowledge, which still informs homoeopathy. They maintained that the whole world was made of these substances or elements and said that human beings were the microcosm within the macrocosm. People today might describe themselves, in simple terms, as having a living physical body. They would acknowledge having feelings and thoughts, and that the combination of the whole is directed and motivated by the individual self.

For the sake of clarity I will, throughout this book, use the terminology of spiritual science, or anthroposophy, as taught by Rudolf Steiner, which describes these four aspects as follows. Firstly there is the *physical*—what we touch, feel and see, which is our *earth body*. Then there is the *life* or *ether* body—the fluid and dynamic chemistry, the *water* of life one might say—which endows the physical matter in the body with living qualities. Permeating all is the *astral* body, or soul, as our feeling, thinking, motivated self, which penetrates everywhere like the *air*. And lastly, the *fire* of the *ego*, which directs and shapes all these substances, making us individual members of the human race, each with our own divine spark, carried and nurtured by our angel.

Earth, water, air and fire live harmoniously in the world, each with its own task but interacting dynamically with the other three.

The soul in relation to destiny

If we accept that the world is a living organism made up of the same intricate, complex substances as the microcosmic human being, we can understand that just as the human ego directs the individual, forging the fourfold human being—as described above—into a unity, there are likewise angels of different ranks who direct and determine cosmic aspects of the macrocosm. Each rank is responsible for its own task within the created world. Nothing is haphazard. Nature and spirit have their laws and follow them. As single individuals we experience the unifying Ego-being of the world, who directs these laws, as the Creator. Ancient religions saw the Creator in the sun or the moon, or in other planetary phenomena, as the one who directs the world and its evolution through time. They also experienced the hand of the gods in their own personal life. Today we say: *I am self-determining, I own my destiny,* whilst simultaneously feeling that there is possibly more than just our narrow selves involved in our progress through life. There are so many occasions where things seem to happen beyond our control.

In moments of despair we ascribe our lack of control over our personal destiny to fate, thinking that destiny and fate are imposed on us from without. Generally, when life becomes harder than we can bear, we long for direction or advice. We find a friend, a counsellor, a close relative, and share our woes and fears. Occasionally, when all fails, we might pray to a higher being, to our guardian angel, or simply to the great goodness that our soul believes to be present somewhere out there. The order and majesty that pervades the natural world suggest to us that a good god exists. Why should such order and majesty not also pervade the individual human soul?

Often, after trying absolutely everything to achieve a desired purpose without success, we find ourselves letting the purpose go, not in the sense of abdication, but simply accepting our powerlessness in a given situation. We hand the issue over to a higher power, as it were. When, as frequently happens in such instances, something changes and a new approach or way forward is found once more, we tend to thank God for small mercies! I believe that most people have had such an experience. I would like to stress that this is a *real occurrence, which we can learn to use as a tool to manage daily life.* We are not, as we imagine, alone and lonely in the universe. We have recourse to our guardian angel who can, and does, offer help and guidance if we are open to learn the language of the spirit.

Our *astral* body, our soul, embodies our ability to think, feel and act, and has the capacity both to learn this language and also to deny its existence. The *ego,* the real self, awakens these skills and directs them. However, if the astral body refuses to listen to the ego's insight, we have a problem. I suspect most people will remember occasions when they have not trusted their own insight and have consequently regretted not listening to their inner voice.

So how can we learn to listen to, trust and act consciously upon the wisdom that the angels offer the soul? How can we commune through the ego, enliven the ether body and bring health to the physical body? Will speaking with angels or other such beings make us less irritable, tired and resentful? If we can accept the existence of our own unique spirit and thereby acknowledge the unique spiritual existence of all other human beings, why is it so difficult to accept the existence of angels except when we are in genuine despair?

Perhaps the reason we often feel so inadequate is because the task of homemaking challenges the astral body, which contains our feeling, thinking, emotions, motives and desires. In our efforts to bring health and well-being into our homes we use, and use up, a great deal of astral qualities. Because our astral body does not only contain our pleasanter aspects but also negative and weak expressions of the self, we are faced with our shortcomings—which is very painful. We need to find a way to help ourselves in this dilemma.

Sleep and destiny

A good night's sleep is something that homemakers most desire and find most refreshing. Children, or others' illness, can interrupt our sleep, and the resulting fatigue can be debilitating.

Why is sleep so important? There are very obvious answers, such as its restorative magic for our physical body, or the lovely opportunity to withdraw from the challenges of daily life. Not only the body and soul recover from the day's activities during the night. The spirit too, the real inner self, seems to rise again after sleep, renewed and ready for action.

During sleep we are unconscious. Nowadays we know that our unconscious is not an absence of consciousness, but merely a different kind of awareness that is frequently more in tune with reality than our conscious intellect. Homemakers in particular will be familiar with the unconscious, intuitive actions they take sometimes in response to a need. These intuitions are often more reliable than our considered thoughts. However, they can also lead to consequences for which we feel unprepared. This is because they come from somewhere deep inside and sometimes take us by surprise.

Intuition is knowledge that we do not know, in our everyday thinking, that we have. It comes to us at night from that place and those beings whom we meet when we sleep. During sleep our body and life forces lie in bed, being cared for by the angelic world. Nowadays, people tend to think that either there are no such beings as angels or that angels are only there to answer our prayers. In fact, if we seriously ask ourselves about our simultaneous material and spiritual existence we will find that the non-material is as real as the material, and that the body goes on living during sleep whilst 'I' am outside it because of non-material beings known as angels who take care of it, replacing 'me'. Meanwhile, my soul and spirit are free to roam the world of spirit in which 'I' recognize and remember my destiny, which I consequently re-experience during the day.

Some people remember past lives. It appears from these accounts that each of us makes a plan for our current life between death and a new birth, according to how we lived our previous life on earth. We forget our 'plan' at birth, but during sleep we can reconnect to it.

Imagine not sleeping for days or months! Sleep deprivation drives the human being mad. One can no longer retain a sense of self, or continuity of self, and nor, consequently, make sense of daily life, of relationships, or tasks. Life becomes a meaningless torment. Mothers of young babies suffering from colic at night will understand what it means to be regularly deprived of sleep and the resulting sense of irrationality and purposelessness.

Sleepless nights may at times be inevitable. At such moments we need an alternative to sleep that can connect us again to our real selves. We are born with an unconscious knowledge of our destiny with which we reunite every night in sleep. When we awaken, our soul and spirit are filled once more with the real purpose of our existence, the reason that we are where we are, doing what we do. We experience this knowledge as renewed energy and enthusiasm for life and work. If we want to manage our daily life with a continuous flow of such energy, meditation or meditative exercises can shape our soul, emotions and thoughts in such a way that we can regain a healthy relationship with our destiny and place in the world. Real meditation is as refreshing as sleep.

Perhaps the simplest way to understand the need for meditation is to imagine that we face a problem with no apparent resolution. Intuitively we know we need time, a space, in which to allow the problem to sink down and be digested. Many people will ask for time to sleep on a question before having to answer it. And often, miraculously, the answer arrives the following morning. It may not be always so instantaneous. It may require a few nights before the answer surfaces, and we may wonder where it has come from. Sometimes we can even wake up with words ringing in our ears, telling us what to do. Who advises us? Who takes care of our unconscious knowledge and pushes it up into clear thoughts or new energy when we need it? Can we arrive at the same clear insight by means of meditation?

Little children sometimes talk about someone next to them, or behind them, who shines with light, protecting them. We know of these beings either through myths and legends from the past, or maybe even from personal experience. Many people today are waking up to the astonishing fact that they have a guardian angel to whom they can talk and who knows their innermost secret hopes and fears.

Angels

Angels are described in many ways. They are depicted in great works of art. They always seem to have wings and to radiate light. To the human imagination, wings denote the ability to fly far, fast and high, which are attributes given also to our thoughts. Our thinking can take us anywhere on the earth and beyond. We can think the unthinkable as well as the invisible. These are qualities of light. In our language we talk about 'shedding light' on things that are hidden or secret, or not easily understood.

Just as my real self is invisible as a material, provable entity, and yet I know myself to be real, so are angels invisible to the material eye, yet equally real to the spiritually active self. It is my real spiritual self that gains consciousness when my material, everyday self goes to sleep. This happens also in meditation. When I am awake in the day, I am asleep in the spirit. When I am asleep in my bed, I am awake in the spiritual world, talking with angels as I talk with my friends during the day.

Angels know the real destiny of a human being in its entirety, because they do not live in time as we human beings do. They behold the totality of each human being's intentions. So when I sleep, I behold my intentions in their entirety through the eyes of my angel. This is very exciting and energizing. I wake up in the morning with the will to do better, to do my best. And as the day passes I use up this spiritual food, gradually forgetting what my angel showed to me—and so I get tired and need to sleep again.

Our angels are always with us, accompanying and protecting us as we go through our life, assisting us gently to follow our true intentions, which we call our destiny. Of course, each one of us has our own destiny peculiar to us. And each one of us has our very own angel. Thus in a home of more than one person, more than one angel is active. One might say that this is the fundamental reason for our differences, the challenge that makes daily life so interesting to the homemaker. For it is in the small actions of ordinary daily life, as much as in public words or deeds, that we can fulfil our destiny. Recognizing that an angel is there to accompany us and help us makes the task spiritually as well as physically satisfying.

Homemaking in daily life

Homemaking always deals with the stuff of daily life in relation to the life of other people; and life is not simple. There may not be any definitive answers, but there are definite methods for finding an inspiring relationship to daily life. A clearly marked path on which we embark can help us learn to understand ourselves better. However, signposts merely state the desired objective, and standing beneath them is not the same as reaching a destination! But it does help to know what we are aiming for. We can all recognize that the homemaker herself is the prime focus in the task of homemaking—the mover and shaker as it were. Yet it is a constant challenge to understand one's true inner being. How I think I affect other people and life itself can be very different from how another person experiences me.

It is difficult to assess oneself, to put oneself into another person's shoes, or to experience the self objectively. We need a yardstick that is universal to all human beings, against which to measure the self. And after the assessment comes the need for a real will for change, and a viable solution to the problems at hand. Wanting to change is not enough. Only deep insight can be a strong enough motivator, plus the self-discipline to work at it, day after day. Old habits die hard.

The seven life processes

There are many ways to understand the human being. For the homemaker, learning to identify and work with the seven life processes can be very useful. Homemaking itself, as a daily task, utilizes these processes in the everyday environment. We can get to know ourselves better by the way in which these processes are active in our soul, our body and in the manner in which we act throughout our daily life. By identifying which of these processes works most—or least— in our soul, we can pave the way for new habits. Thus we strengthen, enliven or subdue a particular process so that it can start to work in a more helpful way.

The seven processes inform all life, energize it and shape it. All seven are essential, all mutually interact, and yet are independent. By learning to identify each one, we discover that they influence our moods, experiences, actions, reactions and thinking. We need to understand them clearly so that we can begin to work effectively on the personal changes we wish to make.

The seven life processes are etheric activities: continuously evolving states, that move dynamically between our astral and ether bodies, partaking of both, stirring *activity* in the soul and *enlivening* the life forces in the physical body. They are wonderfully versatile and creative processes.

When we know what they are and how they work, we can activate each life process in its weaving dynamic between ether and astral activity. We can do so without direct awareness, especially when we are in a healthy and balanced state in body, soul and spirit. When we experience our soul, emotions, drives and desires as unbalanced, then we likewise influence the life processes unconsciously but often to our own detriment. However, we also know that we can take control of, or shape, our emotions, feelings, thoughts and actions.

When we are physically unwell we go to a doctor, knowing we may not be able to heal ourselves. But when our soul is out of kilter we can do something about it by ourselves. First, however, we need to identify the weakness and its cause. We can help ourselves if we discover the primary source of the problem. Only then can we find a real solution.

The seven life processes are: *breathing, warming, nourishing, secreting, maintaining, growing* and *reproducing*. It does not take too great a stretch of the imagination to understand that life itself involves all these processes. We breathe in air and with the air we become conscious of our environment. We develop our own body temperature, which keeps us active and effective in the world around us. We eat and drink, utilizing the nourishment that the earth provides. We digest the food, drawing energy from all that is nutritious; and so we grow and can eventually reproduce. Without breathing we die. Without generating our own warmth organism we need medical intervention. Without food and drink we starve. Without the capacity to digest we would likewise die. If we cannot absorb the nutrients in our food, we waste away, neither growing nor able to reproduce.

As the seven life processes move between our life body and soul, they engender activity in our astral body. For example, when our hormones are stimulated this affects our mood. We attribute many of our mistakes to 'that time of the month'. Or the need to take charge, to be in control overcomes us, our adrenaline dictating our actions. But what if meditative exercises could bring our hormonal moods under our own control, as well as other issues connected with haphazard and fluctuating emotions?

Meditative exercises as self-help tools

A simple and correct conclusion to draw from all the above is that daily problems besetting us in the home all lie in *how* we relate to our own astral body. This affects *how* we approach and manage our tasks.

I came to this conclusion fairly early on in my home-making but it has taken the rest of the 40 years to discover real and tangible remedies. I found I had to arrive at the point of *wanting* to curb or change my natural emotions and habits of thinking and feeling. Most difficult of all was the effort to remodel my instinctive and often damaging reactions to events and to other people's habits.

In reply to my despairing cry for help, a very wise old doctor told me: 'Reform begins at home.' At the time I was, needless to say, not very impressed! But I had the grace to think about it, and when I took the words literally a light shone into the darkness of my burdened soul.

'Reform' means to thoroughly reshape, presumably not in an identical fashion to the previous form. I love homemaking because, although always at somebody else's beck and call, or fulfilling an objective need, I am actually my own boss. It is always within the power of the homemaker herself *how* she responds to, or initiates, or reacts to the tasks in hand.

People react differently to the challenges that life throws at them but there is no doubt that we do react. I saw the challenge of reforming my thinking, feeling and manner of dealing with life's little irritations as the greatest opportunity. So began years of observation of the common problems and challenges that homemakers complain about. Drawing help from insights I gained into both the environmental activity of the seven life processes and the way they weave in the human being's astral and ether bodies, it was not long before I saw that my ego was the obvious place to start.

What do *I* really think? How do *I* feel? What are *my* reactions? Self-assessment is the starting point of reform. When I set out on the path, I soon noticed that some silly things that used to drive me mad ceased to do so. This experience sent me in search of meditation as the key to balancing my soul.

Next it became clear that a homemaker does not have much time for serious meditation and, moreover, often gets interrupted just when she has emptied her mind! So could there be another way to find a source of inner peace, a wellspring of inspiration to hone and focus astral forces?

Throughout the ages people have sought help from meditative exercises when they wished to change themselves, gain control of their lives, or work effectively in the world. These exercises address the soul's balance and poise: the way in which the ego influences the astral, the soul and self inhabit the ether body, and how all that I am lives harmoniously in my physical body. Different exercises influence different aspects and have their own desired result. However, all of them demand the motivation of *personal decision* and *regular practice*.

Exercising implies repetition and training so that whatever one is exercising becomes a habit and need no longer cause stress or pain. To learn an instrument means to practise until the body knows by itself how to play the instrument. Fitness training builds up muscular abilities that make running easy because one is in practice.

Meditative exercises build new soul habits, new qualities of thinking, feeling and reacting. The medium that moves the soul are the seven life processes in their astral manifestation. Exercising strengthens or subdues them, so that they inform or *reform* our life body, which in turn gives balance and health to our physical body.

Hindrances (or personal faults and failings) to harmony of soul come in different guises, depending on which life process needs strengthening or subduing. Different processes require different exercises. Once we can establish a clear understanding of the functions of the processes, we see the influence they have on our soul, and can begin to work creatively and actively with them. However, we need to be able to recognize which process works too strongly or is too weak. Then we need to identify an exercise that will build up or subdue—and then start to practise.

The lovely thing about such practice is that most meditative exercises do not require us to remove ourselves from daily life. They are usually ongoing activities that help us manage daily events as they come and go. They are best set in motion first thing in the morning and reflected upon last thing at night before going to sleep. At these moments of changing consciousness we are closest to a real and tangible contact with our guardian angel. For this reason, the exercises I am recommending will always be connected to the morning and evening, except where they require more alert, waking consciousness.

To assist the reader in identifying which life process she thinks needs attention, I have listed daily life challenges relating to each of the processes. These hindrances come about when a specific process is not functioning very well. This is often caused by life circumstances, but is equally often self-inflicted.

The following chapters will describe the nature of each life process, the aspect of soul it relates to, the positives and negatives it awakens, the potentials that lie in the astral body and the relevant exercises. No doubt one could adopt many more exercises than those I have chosen. However, I hope that those identified in this book, which have also been tried and tested by homemakers other than me, will bring daily challenges into perspective as *opportunities* for self-development, as well as offering solutions to daily life problems.

How to use this book

I must however end this chapter on a note of warning. The following pages describe many exercises, and it would be counter-productive to try to manage all of them at the same time.

Though you will find similarities in many of the exercises, each specifically addresses the life process to which it relates. The life processes *influence* each other, sometimes even overlapping, each one working to enhance the other's activity. Meditative exercises also do this. While they may all seem similar, they differ in small, apparently insignificant ways. These tiny differences stimulate the soul in a tangible way. Choose carefully what you feel is right for you, feeling free to move from one to another as appropriate.

It is a good idea to read through the book as initial exploration and overview, and try to discover where your weaknesses lie, and what inner changes you want to make. Then choose one particular exercise and practise it over a period of time until you feel you have mastered it.

If the exercise becomes a habit, that is very good, as long as it is a conscious one. Should it become a habit without fulfilment, then stop that exercise and choose another. This means starting all over again. But it will take less time to build up a relationship to the new exercise.

You will feel drawn to particular exercises according to your age, life experience, and the type of situation you are currently experiencing. These, of course, change and metamorphose. You will probably find you want to take up different exercises to suit different occasions.

Because we are all different and have different problems rooted in the seven life processes, it is important to identify which process holds the key to your particular challenge and question, because the solution lies hidden in that process. So take your time, don't hurry, but feel confident.

The qualities described in the conclusions are the strengths we gain by practising the exercises contained in the relevant chapter. Meditative exercises offer real possibility for change.

2
Restoring Balance

Breathing

Every homemaker I have met seeks the magic of equilibrium. To be able to meet life's ups and downs, its stresses and strains, in a peaceful and measured mood would be the most desirable thing of all to achieve. But sadly we run around in search of this state of soul, and this running itself drives it further away from our grasp. Reacting to this stress, we sit back and say to ourselves that it doesn't matter anyway, life can go its own sweet way and we will just tag along behind, picking up the pieces as we go along. But that doesn't work either because, sooner or later, we find ourselves lagging so far behind in our plans and aspirations that a feeling of hopelessness or depression can result.

Luckily, almost like a gift from the gods, we have those heaven-sent moments when everything converges in just the right way. By some magical good luck we find we are in control of our lives and events. This perfect balance feels like serendipity. But is it possible to achieve such moments consciously and regularly? Is it possible to create harmony between self and the world?

The *life process of breathing* is what marries soul and world, and can serve as our example here. We breathe in and out from the moment of birth to the moment of death. Breathing is a rhythmical activity of expanding and contracting, taking in air, using its life-bringing substances, and returning it to the world. Used-up air in a room is very unpleasant. Being in a stuffy atmosphere inhibits clear thinking, so that we become muzzy and dull-witted. The moment we open a window and let the fresh air in, our brain clears and we become fully alert again. It is as though the whole world floods in and cleans our consciousness for fresh thinking. Breathing is the foundation of consciousness.

Just as we breathe in and out rhythmically, our attention also has a fluctuating dynamic as we focus on something and then let it sink down into our unconscious. Thankfully, we are not fully conscious of everything all the time. We know that being unable to forget leads to obsession, as though we cannot relax and shut down our thoughts. We cannot breathe out, as it were, but are always breathing in, which is very exhausting.

We have regular times of sleep, when our breathing slows and becomes deep pools of peace. Real sleep makes it possible to fulfil daytime activities. Waking and sleeping are a breathing rhythm, as necessary as air for our welfare.

This rhythm is a change of perspective. We say that when

awake we are fully conscious and when asleep we are unconscious. However, we also know that this unconsciousness is not non-existence. So we can assume that waking and sleeping are merely *different states of awareness.* We are able to work, think, feel, act and react in the world around us when awake. But when asleep we cannot do these things. Our body lies in bed, relaxing and recharging.

When we are stressed or anxious, we go to sleep and wake up feeling stale, still tense and anxious. If this persists we may even find it impossible to sleep. Without sleep, our thoughts and actions get muddled and weary. We can no longer think clearly and so we become depressed. Even though we may lie down in bed all night, we do not feel refreshed at all.

Sometimes, when we feel strong and at ease with ourselves, we consciously decide to go to sleep with a prayer or a direct appeal to a higher being. Then we often wake up with more courage and better heart to face the difficulty, and find its resolution in the course of time.

These examples show that something definitely occurs in us while we sleep. Through an unconscious knowledge of the world we process events which we 'breathed in' with our perceptions during the day. We work through them with the help of higher beings—those non-material, invisible angelic companions who are so much wiser than our waking conscious selves. Day-consciousness brings us knowledge of the world. Night-consciousness brings us knowledge of the self. With each inbreath and outbreath we re-enact in microcosm the rhythm of waking consciousness and night-consciousness. You might say that each inbreath and outbreath is a tiny waking and sleep.

When we speak—for which we need to breathe in and then vocalize on the outbreath—we first make contact with the world, then share our innermost secrets with it. And whenever we listen to the world, which carries its information to us on waves of air as sound, we drink up the innermost secrets of the world.

The balance between speaking and listening can pose a genuine problem for homemakers. Am I withdrawing into my own space when listening? Am I going out towards my fellow human beings when speaking? In point of fact, when I speak I am fully engaged in *projecting myself*. And when I listen, I am fully involved *in the person* to whom I am listening. Throughout our waking day we alternate between this give and take, each in our own particular, personal rhythm.

We live in rhythms that we adapt to our character and lifestyle. And in the same way our process of breathing adjusts our rhythms to enhance our life forces and our soul's needs. It does this by making us feel tired or feel full of energy. Our guardian angel is deeply interested in our life on earth. The degree to which we work with our angel, whether consciously or unconsciously, is measured by our feelings of energy or exhaustion. However, as conscious, self-determining beings we sometimes override messages that the angel sends our soul through the life process of breathing; and then problems arise, such as stress, depression or burn-out. It is not only our environment that causes these problems. It is, in fact, more often ourselves who refuse to breathe rhythmically or live in a rhythmical and therefore balanced way.

Changing the rhythm of our breathing changes our consciousness. We do this quite naturally and without thought. If we get tired we slow down, take a deep breath and have a rest. Or if we are over-charged with energy we do some really hard work, breathing faster to burn up the excess. Our senses perceive occurrences and tell our breathing to change its rhythm to suit the needs of the circumstances. Thus it follows that there must be a close connection between the process of breathing and the sensitivity of the body. Breathing and perceiving are close brothers.

Perceiving

Perceiving is the soul's breathing. As our senses take in the world around us, we build inner pictures, sounds and forms, which we use as the foundation of thinking. Breathing wakes up the ether and physical bodies, and perceiving wakes up the thinking soul. Our physical senses perceive the world and all that is in it. Our soul receives the impressions these make, and also the invisible moods, thoughts and reactions that move in other people's souls, and which stir us to reciprocate. So if we sense unhappiness, anger or fear, we react.

The activity of conceptualizing, which we will discuss in the next chapter, depends entirely on our ability and skills of perception. We perceive all the time, consciously or unconsciously as long as we are alive, just as we breathe throughout our lifetime.

This suggests that we perceive far more than we realize. Perceiving also makes us tired, just like too much speaking or working. The soul can get tired just like the physical body. Tiredness from too much unconscious perception gives rise to the experience of stress and burn-out. No one gets stressed by physical activity. In fact, regular physical exercise *relieves* stress. A commonly recommended remedy for stress is to jog, work-out, swim, walk, etc. Stress is actually pressure from too many perceptions, which we cannot transform into concepts. They just sit there, unused and unwanted, sapping a great deal of our life forces, which in turn affects our physical health and well-being.

Regular practice of meditative exercises helps us to work rhythmically with our faculty of perceiving and establish a healthy soul-breathing rhythm. Learning to work on the activity of perceiving requires something other than normal housekeeping duties. It requires an understanding of the fundamental qualities that compose our astral body.

Sympathy and antipathy

The soul, or astral body, is a complex entity. It encompasses our emotions, thoughts, feelings, instincts, perceptions, etc., each quality working in its own specific way and interacting with all the other aspects. It is colourful, cheerful, angry, sad, negative, positive—a body of contradictions and paradoxes. We can all recognize that we are complex beings, by no means always logical and yet always working towards becoming a better person.

Fundamental to the contradictions inherent in us are two distinct, *opposing* faculties that we call sympathy and antipathy. In sympathy we share feeling with something. In antipathy we feel opposed to something. We often judge ourselves as a better or worse person depending on how much we are able to sympathize or to what extent we develop antipathy.

But if we examine these faculties more closely, we may find that sympathy can be as negative a reaction as antipathy. We do not like ourselves when we reject someone, but nor do we feel good about condoning everything as acceptable. We recognize that we need to weigh up events, people, circumstances, before we can make a useful decision. Therefore it follows that sympathy and antipathy are neither negative nor positive qualities, but both are essential faculties we need to make informed judgements.

When something occurs, we would all prefer to react wisely, but sometimes our immediate sympathy makes us do unwise things; and equally, immediate antipathy can make us do different, but also unwise things. Sympathy and antipathy are the forces that can keep us in balance once we begin to understand our personal relationship to each one. To develop the ability to look at ourselves with clear eyes, we need the power of antipathy. To accept ourselves and our mistakes, and keep trying to do better, we need the power of sympathy.

We may know these qualities better as subjectivity and objectivity. When I feel sympathetic, I immediately immerse myself in what I feel drawn to, and can lose myself in it, becoming entirely subjective. When I feel antipathy, I can turn away from the event and become cold, hard-hearted and totally detached—a requirement for objectivity. My thinking is involved in controlling and balancing my feelings of sympathy or antipathy, and my greater subjectivity or objectivity.

To sum up, sympathy and antipathy are inborn soul qualities, neither good nor bad, simply barometers of my capacity to feel. Subjectivity and objectivity are those same forces influenced by my own capacity for thinking, and can therefore be good or bad depending on my mood, education, selfishness, needs, etc.

In order to manage homemaking, the way one works with sympathy and antipathy, with objectivity and subjectivity, constantly affects one's actions. No doubt everyone can sympathize with the feeling of helplessness that overcomes us at times and can make us react by forcing control over things that might well have been no trouble to us if we could only have left them to develop in their own way. Homemakers can sometimes become meddlers! And homemakers can also sometimes become cold-hearted managers.

Meditative exercises for breathing and perceiving

There are three approaches that restore balance and thus bring health to those who feel they are suffering from stress, depression or imminent burn-out. They are taking time to perceive events accurately, refraining from drawing instant conclusions, and working on the premise that your angel is working with you. Other homemakers and wise advisers suggested them to me and, having worked with them, I have come to experience and appreciate their vast potential. The following exercises are all quite simple at first and in their simplicity are not difficult to practise. But like many apparently simple things, their complexity develops with familiarity. Once you have begun one or the other practice according to choice, you can feel how you develop self-confidence, inner peace and harmonious interaction with those with whom you live and work.

Reverence

Nowadays, reverence has an old-fashioned ring to it. We see ourselves down on our knees before a great and powerful god. But in venerable, bygone days reverence was a genuine comfort. God *was*. He ruled, and life was ordered by destiny.

Today, we forget the wonder of Creation. We know ourselves as self-motivated individuals. We live in a civilization much of which is, indeed, man-made. But we often forget that what human beings have created was once a thought in someone's mind. Where do our thoughts come from? We can gain the impression that they come from somewhere other than ourselves, or surface deep within our souls. Thoughts are a great gift to humanity from higher beings. In particular, thoughts relating to our personal destiny come to us from our guardian angel.

Without reverence for the created world and the universality of thoughts we lose our connection to reality. I am part of the natural world, which feeds, sustains and delights my whole being. In the spiritual activity of thinking I participate in the totality of all spiritual beings.

Small children approach life and all that is around them with utter reverence. When a little child presents you with a worm, he is filled with wonder and awe. Our reactions, of course, depend on how much reverence we feel for life. But if we can say with true feeling: 'How wonderful! Now let the little creature go to his true home, in the soil,' the child will return the worm unharmed, and know that the world is filled with undiscovered treasures.

Reverence is an inner attitude that brings hope and joy. To live with reverence in thought, word and deed is not as difficult as it may seem. We gradually learn to see that everything is precious and worth our love, and this can imbue our work with a spiritual quality. With reverence, the world becomes a friend and helper.

The practice is as follows.

On awakening, remind yourself of the quality of reverence, and that you want to fill your day with this inner attitude.

Before going to sleep, assess honestly how you got on with it.

Neither of these actions need take any time at all. They must however, be honest and heartfelt. And they should be practised *every morning and every night*. The regularity of preparation and assessment are as essential as inbreath and outbreath.

No doubt at first you will often find you have failed. Your child got up earlier than you and made a huge mess. Did you manage to revere his creativity and help him tidy up? Or did you get cross?

Assessment does not mean to judge yourself harshly but merely to observe honestly and, having observed, to decide to try again and hopefully do better. And if you were successful, even if only on one occasion during the day, simply acknowledge it, but don't rest on your laurels. Gradually, over time, reverence for all will become a new habit of soul, influencing your thinking and making your actions peaceful and in tune with events, not least because your perceptions will be true and accurate. You will no longer react thoughtlessly.

Reverence is like taking a deep breath of fresh air. Perceptions become clear pools of water for the thirsty soul. And so when tricky or painful or contentious issues arise, the first reaction may not be to fight back but rather to take a sip of reverence, seeing the event in a different light.

Taking note

If reverence sounds too difficult, you can start by making a resolution to note *one moment* in the day where you encountered something good, beautiful or true. It may be as small as the first primrose in spring, or a smile from a stranger, or a sentence in a book. Cherish it. It lightens the soul and deepens the breathing. The morning preparation and the evening assessment are still essential activities. In time, reverence will grow and you will be able to take the steps described above.

Beholding

Here we have another old-fashioned word, but I hope you will soon see that it is a thoroughly modern and relevant activity. Beholding means to see something without judgement, without feeling the need to change it in any way. To behold implies putting yourself at a distance from what you behold yet still 'holding' it in your soul, understanding and totally accepting its existence. Beholding brings peace to the soul. You simply acknowledge that what happens or is, has its own justification.

There are times in life at home when things can get fraught, when situations get out of hand and you end the day feeling frazzled, disrespected, annoyed with yourself and others. You can get into conflict with other members of the house community, disagreeing with them on just about anything.

The best time to practice beholding is just before going to sleep. Allow the difficulty to pass before your mind's eye. Simply behold it, reserving judgement, without mental commentary. Then offer the picture to your angel *and to the angel of the other person/people involved in your predicament.* Conclude by saying words to the effect: *Not my will, but thy will be done.* Then go to sleep.

You might say that sleep will be impossible after becoming so conscious of your problem. On the contrary, by making the effort to behold, you actually offer up your challenge for a higher being to behold, who receives it as a gift. Angels do not understand literal words but rather the mood of soul that enthuses the words, giving them inner meaning.

It is not uncommon that a solution offers itself after only one attempt at beholding, if only because you wake up more relaxed and less troubled by the issue. You are thus able to meet the people concerned with a more objective attitude, your angel using your faculty of antipathy to help you to step a little outside of the equation.

It may take several nights, or perhaps only one, but a resolution will arise in you, and the need to blame another will fade.

Beholding people

Beholding can be practised as a positive force for peace. Every night before going to sleep, behold the members of your house community in a moment where each was at his best. Offer the picture to your angel and each person's angel, and let it go. Do the same again but now behold a moment when each was at their worst. Offer the picture and say the words: *Not my will, but thy will be done.* And go to sleep.

It takes no time at all to behold someone. Just by thinking of them they flash before your inner vision. It is best not to try to hold on to the picture even if it is funny or sweet. Simply move on to the next picture or to the next part of the exercise. The moment you hang on, judgements will creep in and sully the angels' vision, closing your soul to their gaze.

Beholding requires regularity just like inbreath and out-breath. Beholding activates the power of perceiving accurately, and thus offers healing to the soul.

If you have difficulty in believing in angels the exercise still works. The soul's ability to let go of an issue allows it to relax and open up to new possibilities. This gives angels access. An angel helps, whether we believe it or not!

Review

Homemakers are very familiar with multi-tasking. We can sometimes feel as if we have to be in three different places at once. Whilst busy doing certain chores, our minds are busy with other things that need doing. We need to plan ahead, get things done, care for each person and everything within the home. We may justifiably feel like a stretched elastic about to snap.

Addressing this problem requires a little more time than the previous exercises. Before going to sleep, sit in a chair with a candle burning or a dim light in the room so that you will not fall asleep.

Review your day *backwards*, starting with the moment you sat down, and review your day in reverse until the morning when you woke up.

At first this may seem quite impossible. You will probably fall asleep in your chair before your review reaches the moment you brushed your teeth five minutes ago! Once you can stay awake a little longer, you will probably get stuck on an event and find yourself rehashing a million other things that relate to the event.

My advice is: start simply. Try to review the main

headings, as it were, and get them in the proper reverse order. Once you can do this smoothly (and it may take weeks), start to review one or the other event as you get to it in more detail. After some years you may become very good at this reverse review.

The real purpose of this meditative exercise is to train one's perceptions. It is wonderful if you can do the exercise perfectly, but that is a distant goal. The attempt itself, the effort expended, is the really important and transformative thing. Each evening you say to yourself: *I will start again.*

Preview

When you wake up in the morning, having set the time on your alarm clock for five minutes before you need to get up, lie in your bed and let the new day register in your mind. Survey the known events that are to take place in the coming day, imagining them peacefully unfolding as the hours pass.

Let the pictures go and say: *I will deal with things as they come. They will come to meet me.*

By previewing in this manner, you can develop the strength to adjust to the surprises that happen almost every day in the life of a homemaker; your response to them will be natural and flexible, without stretching you to your limits.

Equilibrium

Rhythmical breathing is the foundation of equilibrium. Modern life does not naturally supply us with peace. We live at a fast, sometimes driven pace. Our homes too are affected by the pace of life in general. Trying to slow it down does not always work. And opting out, though nice at first, may leave us in financial difficulties.

But fortunately we are thinking, creative beings. We can decide to take on the challenge and find ways to slow ourselves down inwardly. The life process of breathing is our guide. Rhythm in movement, which physical exercise provides, rhythm in our soul, which reverence provides, clarity in our perceptions, which beholding provides, and training our perceptions to be accurate, which the review stimulates, all contribute to approaching our life with ease and grace. The preview gives us the confidence to get up each day and start again.

3
Discovering Understanding

Warming

The members of the house community themselves require the most attention in the home. Everyone is different of course, and it can take an enormous effort of imagination and inspiration to manage all the differences harmoniously. We can use up a great deal of energy in frustration and desperation generated by our own inability to completely understand what is going on inside another person's head or heart. Homemaking would seem to demand a degree in psychology!

Naturally, it's better to approach tricky issues with love. We would really like to approach them with care and understanding too. Love can be a little too much at times, its intensity repelling. Tact, warmth and directness all need to blend, in order to tackle another person's problem, especially if you are bound up in the dilemma. Living together with others is usually based on affection. We live with our families or with friends. Sometimes, in communities built on intention, we might live with perfect strangers who gradually become our friends. But we probably would not live under the same roof in the same household for very long if we did not find a common basis for understanding and cooperation.

The *life process of warming* is a faithful helper in getting to know one another. We always hope to create a warm and friendly environment, shying away from a cold, over-intellectual, analytical atmosphere. We begin the process of getting to know one another carefully and slowly. Of course it can happen that there is an instant rapport, but it can happen just as often that this suddenly evaporates, and we are left with a feeling of betrayal. Without doubt, the slow but steady discoveries build a more solid foundation.

It is also possible that what began as instant dislike can turn into a reliable and valuable friendship, if we give each other the benefit of the doubt. Somehow, the effort it takes to warm to each other, a gentle and careful interaction, builds a real and lasting understanding.

We all know that once a friendship or relationship is made it may not endure without continuous cultivation and renewal. We have to keep the fire burning. And the more we understand each other, the more gently and reliably the embers glow. This requires commitment—something that we need to decide and carry out.

Physically, the life process of warming is found in the bloodstream, as well as in the internal and external movements of the body. Blood is warm because it moves. Where there is movement, there is warmth. And within the warmth of the bloodstream, which flows into every part of our body (even the minutest), the intentions of the real self can find a relationship to our actions. When our body is cold it is far more difficult to move, to do things and to be in touch with our environment.

The centre of movement is the heart. It moves in an eternal rhythm stimulated by the process of breathing and impelled by the flow of blood. And when our heartbeat speeds up, it is either because we are exerting ourselves or because we are agitated. We can experience a rapid heartbeat when we are angry, or when we anticipate something or when we love with passion. Our moods alter our heart's rhythm. Our moods also alter the effect we have on our environment, especially on our fellow human beings.

When dealing with other people we cannot really afford simply to react according to our moods. We know that what we most dearly long for is equanimity, that quality which enables us to act appropriately, feel appropriately and think constructively rather than merely reacting or planning every action in advance. In our heart of hearts, we long to meet challenges with warmth and understanding and, should it become necessary, to turn away the problem with a loving gesture, rather than dismissing it out of hand. We also do not want to become part of a dilemma unnecessarily and undeservedly, simply because we have become too embroiled in it.

The process of warming is our internal boundary builder. If I warm to something, I reach out from my heart to understand, absorbing back into my heart what is revealed to me for understanding.

However, this ideal is not easy to achieve because each of

us has our own special degree of warmth and our very own individual way of expressing it. The warmth of our emotions is coloured by our temperament. We may have a fiery personality, quick to judge and quick to forgive. We may be cool as a still pool, reflecting the world and its events before acting. We may be delightfully flexible and equally delightfully forgetful. And we may take on every sorrow and woe, sometimes even seeking them out. These four basic constitutional approaches to life are called: *choleric, phlegmatic, sanguine and melancholic.*

Our basic temperament informs our moods; and unless the real, eternal ego holds sway over our temperament, the latter will dictate the way we respond to every occurrence. This is not to say that being a choleric, or a melancholic, is a bad thing. Each temperament has its gifts to bring to our endeavour to live a loving life. In principle we can rejoice in the temperaments, at the same time recognizing that they are rooted in the physical body and ether body, working upwards into the astral body. It is here that we can begin to change them by working consciously with the life process of warming that permeates our soul. We can begin to shape them, cultivating a better balance between the four than our nature may originally have endowed us with. To stimulate the warmth of soul we need to work on our temperament, we need to consider our concepts. How do we form them? Are they accurate, factual and based on reality?

Conceptualizing

When we absorb a perception and *think about it*, it becomes a concept alive in our soul. As long as the impression remains unconscious, it cannot connect to anything other than itself and remains a perception. It sinks into the ether body as a picture only, becoming a concept when *I* draw it up and connect it to another perception. My *activity* of connecting gives the perception meaning and thus I form a concept. In so doing, I become aware of myself in relation to the world. If we look objectively at the concepts we form, we find they are coloured not only by our thinking but also by our temperament.

Interacting with the world happens all the time, unconsciously and consciously. That so much is registered unconsciously can be illustrated by the common experience of knowing something and feeling surprised to find that we know it. A new event reveals the perception that lay dormant in us as a picture to connect with the present occurrence. We call this 'life experience'. We form concepts more often than we realize.

So much happens in life that we note down without really noticing. Oddly enough, these concepts are usually sound and can be relied upon when they rise up out of our unconscious. Perhaps they are so true because we have not personalized them as much as those concepts and beliefs that we form consciously.

The things that we notice are the things that affect us. And generally we form concepts based on liking and disliking. Sometimes, concepts are based on our mood at the time, which we failed to observe. These concepts are entirely personal and sometimes not very accurate.

It is important to understand that we base our judgements on our concepts. And so it can happen that, because I am choleric, I form my concepts passionately and too quickly. The actions that follow may not be helpful. Or, if I am phlegmatic, my concepts are formed slowly and my reactions may be delayed. A sanguine person will flit from concept to concept, easily making judgements and decisions and just as easily reversing them. The melancholic, however, will ponder and worry, turning her concepts over and over till she may no longer know what to think.

The astral body is a wonderfully rich and varied ground for the ego to work upon. It gives us the possibility to change ourselves, our actions, our thoughts and feelings, because it contains a myriad of potential. With a warm heart we can build bridges between the self and the world, the self and the other, by recognizing that every human soul has the very same potential as we ourselves. From this can develop greater equanimity and understanding, so that we live with our friends, family and the world in more peace and harmony.

Empathy

Empathy is a much sought-after quality. It is a precious state that does not judge but understands and shares the feelings, thoughts or deeds of another. We all know the magic that enters into difficult situations when empathy is born between people. Suddenly insurmountable differences become tolerable points of view to be discussed and answers found, without losing our own standpoint or compromising our moral stance.

Whatever our basic temperament and outlook, as soon as we understand the other person's point of view we can share in it, without necessarily adopting it. With empathy we step into another person's shoes, seeing and thinking as she does, whilst retaining our own personal view and experience. Some people are naturally very good at this. The free space which empathy creates can allow someone to find their own resolution. However, sometimes further action is needed on both sides. The concepts formed by empathy will always be sound and true, deepening under-standing so that a suggested solution can then also be adopted with freedom of heart and mind. In other words, it does not feel imposed or compelled.

However, we can mistake empathy for sympathy, imagining that if I totally identify with another I will lose my own opinion and adopt theirs. This cannot happen. Empathy is the result of accurate and true conceptualizing. It is like getting a bird's eye view of the world. From up there we can see many aspects simultaneously and grasp their relationship to each other. Empathy can give us this kind of overview of thoughts, feelings and actions, as a map does for a traveller. It gives us the ability to connect concepts of self and other. We acquire this quality when we can withhold our opinions without giving them up, so that the other person's point of view can shine through and together we can see each other clearly.

But the sad fact is that instead we often take sides, seeing things too much from our own, narrower perspective. In an effort not to do so, we use our intellectual, analytical skills to swing back into antipathy. We can orientate with too much detail, examining a minute part of the map without recourse to the whole. Warmth of heart, which may try to make itself felt in order to widen the bound-aries, may consequently appear as sentimentality. Such analysis frequently leads to us going round and round in circles, resulting in tiredness, frustration and a feeling of failure or indifference.

Indifference is hurtful to others and experienced as rejection. The boundaries are drawn too tight. I keep myself in a position that feels safe, and dismiss others to their own separate space. We may not quarrel but we will also not interact with warmth. Real and actual rejection occurs when we have reached a point of not coping with another's impact upon us. Unfortunately, rejection is reciprocal and we will find ourselves poles apart, a chilly gap that neither party actually wants to cross.

Wanting something, on the other hand, is a very warming feeling, sometimes too warm, and in small, apparently insignificant ways our 'wanting' can make us do things we might afterwards regret. Unhappiness, too, is often caused by lack of empathy. We swing too abruptly from mood to mood, from thought to thought, or we fixate ourselves on a thought that was valid once, but, because life keeps changing, is no longer useful. And then we can begin to dislike ourselves, which inevitably leads to disliking others.

Governing our moods and our wants depends upon empathy for others and also for the self. It is extremely counter-productive to condemn, congratulate or to ignore myself. It is good to love oneself whilst also endeavouring to examine personal actions, thoughts and feelings.

To cultivate empathy so that we can think, feel and act with equanimity, we need to learn to form our concepts consciously and, if they have been formed unconsciously, to empathize with them warmly until we can really understand them and, if necessary, correct them. Then we can fulfil our aims with real and loving determination. But as always it takes practice.

Meditative exercises for warming and conceptualizing

Learning to bring our moods, opinions, and judgements under our own control requires us to warm to our faults and failings. Generally, they are not so terrible as to be unforgivable. We would get along so much better with each other if we learnt to rejoice in our differences. It is surprising but frequently true that we appear to want everyone to be 'just like me'! In fact, when we meet a person similar to ourselves, we often find them very irritating, seeing their so-called faults in the mirror of our own failings. We are really most annoyed about something because we recognize it in ourselves. If someone is entirely different, we can like them again because they have qualities we lack and would love to acquire.

Exercises to help in subduing the natural tendencies to judge, to want, to reject, or be too passionate about things always begin with placing yourself in the centre of your efforts.

Contemplation

Here is another lovely, old-fashioned word. To contemplate means to spend time, to ponder upon things. It includes thinking and visualizing and observing, not only the person or event or thing but also yourself in relation to the person or event or thing.

Contemplating needs time. It is necessary to be alone, in peace. This is an essential part of the exercise because you have to remove yourself not only mentally but physically from the hustle and bustle. This helps to find perspective.

Choose any time of the day that suits you to carry out this

exercise. Start by reviewing a moment when things went the way you think was right. It is best to pick out a specific, short moment and try to visualize it clearly. This means looking at it from as many angles as possible, leaving the chance open that there might have been an angle you missed. Very often there is! It is usually the angle connected to how the others experienced you in that moment. As soon as you have discovered this and are able to see yourself in the situation as objectively as possible, you can leave that moment and start on another.

Remember that contemplation does not include judgement. It does, however, ask that you include *yourself*. It is not helpful to contemplate too long. Perhaps five minutes is enough. What is essential is to make the exercise a daily event.

The skill that follows after some time of practice is the ability to observe the truth of what is happening in the moment that it is happening. Don't lose heart if, once you have started, nothing changes in you immediately. Something does begin but perhaps unnoticed by you, though it will be noticed by others. You will find that your reactions will be more acceptable to them, even if not yet perfect.

Contemplating your moods is another helpful exercise. Simply to acknowledge them, to see yourself as they change throughout the day is all that is required. Deep soul-searching is counter-productive. It often leads to self-condemnation or self-congratulation, both of which are a huge distraction from the actual purpose.

Contemplation can, of course be done last thing at night but as one is often very tired, it is best to try to find a time during the day. If it is really impossible to find the time, try the following exercise.

Interest

It is often quite difficult to love everyone and everything. Though we all want to do so, we have to admit that we cannot. There will be things and people whom we do not really love. And we may be required by circumstances to live or work or associate with them. Our options are to ignore them, to avoid them, to fight them, or reject them utterly. This is very painful and affects us deeply in our moods and in our performance, as well as in our energy levels. The ether body is weakened and the astral body gets tight and stiff. We feel this in our physical body as lack of enthusiasm and exhaustion.

To re-energize it is always possible to decide to be interested in things. Who is this person that I cannot warm to? What made the event that I did not enjoy so miserable or boring? Why did I find myself enjoying something which I had not wanted to attend?

Interest engenders warmth of heart and mind. It brings a little flame of enthusiasm into the dullest of things. You can even be interested in why things should ever appear dull! Interest reaches out towards the unknown. It requires a decision to face life with interest but, once made, the most surprising, pleasant, exciting, challenging things may follow. A person who cultivates interest is attractive to others. Interacting with others generates energy.

Moreover, may I recommend being interested in yourself? Why did you do what you did? Why are you often in a bad mood? Why are you afraid of certain things? Why are you drawn to some things and not to others? What makes you tick? Why were you friendly in one situation and unfriendly in another?

To be interested does not require time. It requires the decision to look at life through this attribute, which you consequently put into practice.

Self-examination

Self-examination is very refreshing. I think it may be true to say that all meditative exercises include this practice. At first, you may fall into the trap of assuming that self-examination means to judge yourself. On the contrary, no judgement should arise. But you can draw conclusions provided they are always open to change, and based on correct concepts.

To start with, you may be too hard on yourself because you compare yourself with the perfection from which you fall short. You may fall into the opposite trap of assessing yourself leniently, making excuses for yourself. Don't lose heart. Just keep trying to put aside value judgements, comparisons, blame, congratulations, etc. and examine yourself with the eyes of a stranger who is deeply interested in *you*. Blowing neither hot nor cold, employ the breeze of enthusiasm. When you have come to a conclusion say to yourself: *This was how I was. Tomorrow it will be different.* You may allow yourself to conclude that you could have done better. You may allow yourself to conclude that you did what you did as well as you could. But always leave space for opportunities.

Self-examination is best done last thing at night before going to sleep. Like the review, it opens the door for angelic support and guidance. Unlike the review, it is not necessary to examine every moment of the day. You are free to select whatever you choose as long as it relates to *yourself, your* moods, *your* performance, *your* thoughts and concepts.

The eightfold path

There are seven aspects of life that make or break relationships. Homemakers, like every human being, employ these. They are: *opinions, judgements, speech, actions, moral stance, habits, memories.* All of them can make us take wrong or right decisions. Today, we dislike using the words 'wrong' or 'right'. They seem to be judgemental. This may be so when deciding on behalf of others, but when honestly assessing ourselves we are permitted, and often even helped, by making informed, justly assessed judgements.

To begin with, you must ask the question: 'What is the right opinion, the right judgement, etc. in any given situation? How can I find it?' 'Right' in this context is not a value judgement. It is simply the ability to connect the perceptions of an event to what actually happened so that the resulting concepts are true.

To practise the eightfold path we need to use self-examination as described above so that we can find the 'right' attitude. It is both the first and foremost step on this path, as well as the final and resolving eighth step.

Like all meditative exercises, start slowly and carefully. Begin by working on 'opinion' for a whole month. The next month, take up 'judgement' and so on. When you have practised all the aspects, each for a month, then attach them to the days of the week and practise each in their turn as the days of the week go, as follows:

Saturday: Right opinion
Sunday: Right judgement
Monday: Right word
Tuesday: Right deed

Wednesday: Right moral stance
Thursday: Right habit
Friday: Right memory
Every night: Self-examination

Of course, self-examination at the end of each day will now be focused on the step you are currently exercising.

In practice it goes like this. On waking, remind yourself which step you are pursuing. Resolve to watch your opinions if it is Saturday, your judgements if it is Sunday, etc. and then get up and go about your daily life. In the evening, examine how you got on.

The eightfold path is something to live by. It never ceases to be interesting, stimulating and life changing. It does not require you to remove yourself from life. On the contrary, it asks you to be involved, to live to the full whilst beginning to understand yourself better, consequently understanding others better too.

Tact, patience, empathy, interest, humour, joy, decision-making, all the attributes that make life more liveable will begin to shine within your soul. However, do not think the eightfold path is a quick fix! It is a journey of the soul, one that you can go on without leaving home. It will eventually become as comforting as a much-loved companion.

Equanimity

Every human being is unique. Yet we can recognize the same qualities in every other person that live also in ourselves. We are all subject to faults, and all rejoice in our achievements. We acquire equanimity when the differences cease to irritate us, drawing forth from us negative passions, reactions, judgements and opinions. We can look upon our companions, our life, our work, hopes and aspirations as threads that make the tapestry of life a colourful and warm material that wraps us, displaying to others the path of our destiny, just as their destiny reveals itself to us.

4
Creating Joy

Everyday things that kill joy

Experiencing underlying boredom; obsessing over things; being careless; feeling fearful; avoiding risks; damping down spontaneity; being self-absorbed; being uncommunicative; easily accusing self or others; being self-effacing; being grumpy; dealing badly with surprises; rigidly sticking to plans; saying 'no' before 'yes'; disparaging the unknown; sticking to the familiar; brooding on wrongs; feeling trapped; being set in your ways.

Nourishing

What makes us want to change? What is it that fills us with either dread of life or warms us with vitality and interest, excitement and anticipation of things to come? Why did we choose to become homemakers?

Without doubt, the world is a wonderful place, containing joys and sorrows in equal measure. It is not uncommon to desire only the joys, discarding the sorrows as miserable times to be forgotten as fast as possible. And yet, deep inside, we all recognize that the tough times are often the most developmental.

When difficulties arise we become more aware of a hunger or thirst for wisdom, for knowledge, for skills and abilities that we know we need, not only to survive, but simply to manage the challenges. We can even sometimes bemoan our lack of a particular faculty that we know would assist us in finding a solution to the question or problem. We can think of this feeling as a hunger in the soul that needs to be fed.

The *life process of nourishing* is not only satisfied and stimulated by food. This aspect belongs to our physical body, which needs good, nutritious food to stay alive and be healthy. The ether body and the soul also require nourishment. And when these bodies are satisfied and healthy, the ego can find a relationship to life, the world and to others in a healthy and creative way.

Homemaking is all too often experienced as debilitating routines, with needs and demands sucking up energy and creativity. We can feel starved of culture, space, time, leisure and, most of all, artistic expression. Ask any homemaker and she will tell you that she rarely gets time for hobbies. She is too busy helping someone else in *their* hobbies!

We spend a great deal of time cleaning, cooking, caring, shopping, ferrying people to and fro, and getting thinner and thinner—not physically especially, but certainly in the soul. Some people rebel at this starvation of the self and take up a study or get a job. This will indeed be stimulating but may lead to a different kind of hunger—that of finding soul-space for contemplation, for just simply being alone.

To be really healthy in body, soul and spirit, we need food for body, soul and spirit so that the life process of nourishing can flourish within us. This is true health and satisfactory well-being. Good food for the body, when presented beautifully, also nourishes the soul, and if cooked with love, feeds the spirit. However, there are other things we should pay attention to if we want to really nourish the soul so that the spirit can radiate creatively. The artistic inventiveness of the soul exists entirely in imagination. Images are formed from the world around as well as the world within us. We can absorb facts and simultaneously picture these facts, so that the images live deep inside us, whether as an image of letters, numbers, geometrical patterns or sounds and colours that move and weave. The imagination is always pictorial, alive and in movement. To summon up these pictures we use our memory.

Memory

Imagine having no memory. Life would have absolutely no coherence. Everything would be entirely in the here and now, making no sense without connection to anything other than each immediate sense impression. Luckily we have memory, the ability to draw into the soul all the impressions our senses perceive, letting them sink into the ether body, and allowing them to rest in the muscles and tissues of our physical body.

Then, when we dive down and focus our consciousness, we can resurrect the impressions in pictures, colours, forms, sounds or movements that lie dormant. Memories are evocative, sad, happy, boring—according to our current mood. Memories are rarely accurate representations of events, because at the time of the event they recall we were in a certain state of mind or mood and this impresses itself on us too. So when we take a look at a memory we feel that past mood and impose on it our present mood. Memories change and grow but are always intensely personal. We can even remember something that never happened or experience something someone told us as though it were our own memory.

Impressions come to us through our senses. Unless we are fully and completely alert to what a sense is telling us it simply sinks down into our memory, sleeping until awakened by our thinking or feeling. We might sometimes wonder how we know something, being completely unaware that we read it in passing while driving our children to school.

There are however memory soul pictures, alive in our innermost being, which we have brought with us from before birth. Our angel keeps these pictures nourished for us. Together with our deepest self, the angel draws them up during sleep for the soul and ego to gaze upon and feel once again fed. These pictures are of our intentions, destiny and goals. Such memories feed us and also tug at our consciousness, reminding us that we have come into the world with aims and intentions. However, it is often hard to relate these deep memory pictures to everyday life and thus direct ourselves towards fulfilling those intentions, living out our destiny as we planned it or reaching our goals.

And this leaves us feeling hungry, dissatisfied and at the mercy of daily life problems and challenges. Homemaking then becomes drudgery, an uncreative duty forced upon us.

Creativity

Every person is an artist. Art is not about painting a picture which sells for millions but about expressing the images alive in the soul. It is about finding the spirit in all its beauty embedded and embodied in material things. Our house and home, our garden, our environment is the canvas on which homemakers express their art. Creativity is imaginative thoughts and feelings offered to the glorious world for ourselves and others to perceive and enjoy.

We can express our creativity through very mundane activities. Cleaning and cooking, gardening and maintenance are the paper on which we paint. A clean, gleaming bathroom or kitchen is a beautiful work of art. However, as with all artists, the work is never quite done, so we repeat our efforts daily. Where we differ from other artists is in the fact that at home others take a hand in the work. Sometimes they mess it up, sometimes they enhance an angle or structure. But the homemaker eventually returns to the canvas and adjusts the picture, hopefully appreciating the additions or subtractions someone else has made.

Seeing housework as drudgery dries up our creative talent. We should wake up to a new imaginative thinking. We are entitled to the recognition that we are artists in daily life. Old habits of thought keep us on the straight and narrow path of duty, but we can empower ourselves to become creative within the parameters of our task. Homemaking is varied enough to give countless opportunities for artistic talent.

We would do well to remind ourselves of this startling truth. Art is not merely to paint, sculpt, make music, compose or act in such narrow terms. Every time we cook a meal we create a work of art. Every time we clean and arrange a room, we sculpt space. Every time we move through our daily chores in harmony with the things we use, we make music. And every time we interact imaginatively with our fellow house companions, we are acting on the stage of life.

Luckily our senses constantly remind us of the beauties to be discovered in everyday things. Usefulness is also an aspect of beauty; thus our household tools and domestic appliances have their rightful place too. Our senses are windows of the soul, through which we can look inwards and outwards. We take in soul and spirit food as long as we remember that to live life creatively unites us with angelic creator beings, with our own genius. We need not starve, turning away from the nourishment brought to us by our angel when we sleep.

Creativity is a state of mind, and thoughts have enormous power. How we think can make or break us. We are constantly reminded that a positive attitude to life engenders health and well-being.

However, it is surprising to discover that one can fall into habits of thought as easily as into habits of mood or reaction. Our thinking is not always as free as we would like. It is shaped by our education, upbringing, friends, parents, culture and nationality. Besides, what we may assume to be our own thoughts are often thoughts of others which we have adopted. This is not a negative thing at all. We cannot divorce ourselves from the past, which has made us who we are. But we help ourselves towards freedom and inspiration if we acknowledge our debt to others and use our imagination to understand what our memories show us. Rather than taking on others' views wholesale, we can consciously make them our own or select from them.

We create from the stuff of life, together with other people. Here we cannot allow ourselves to act out of habit, least of all habitual thinking. Everyone is different. It is the differences that make the composition. With imaginative thinking we dive into soul pictures, which angels nourish in us. Children are so much closer to these images, telling us surprising and charming stories they make up, which often contain wisdom beyond their years and experience. This wisdom is alive in us, but we only discover it when we turn our gaze on our soul.

The world of today would have us think logically, analytically and accurately, basing our thoughts on 'facts'. The faculty of the intellect can be used very creatively as long as we apply it to the imaginative pictures we have, without replacing these pictures with dry abstractions. The intellect helps us to bring into physical reality the ideas, images and aims we want to express.

We do not need to starve for lack of inspiration. We only need to become aware that everything we do, feel and think can be either creative or not, according to how we look at it.

Meditative exercises for nourishing and memory

As we get older, the thing we fear most is to lose our memory. We are told to keep an active mind, which helps keep our mental faculties alert. Stimulating creativity not only helps our memory but it also keeps us agile and young at heart.

The routines of life can seem deadening and yet, for a home to run smoothly, routine is a must. Habitual thinking will be no help at all in bringing routine to life. But creative, imaginative thinking transforms routine chores into living, lively activities. We only need to observe our children and what fun they get out of playing 'Mummies and Daddies'! However, we usually need to use a great deal of imagination to get satisfaction from our washing machine, our vacuum cleaner or our fridge. And rushing through the shopping in busy supermarkets with two children in tow requires a concerted effort of imagination to find it stimulating and creative! Living in the present as we do something we dislike can entail the risk of making the chore more disagreeable.

And yet a large part of homemaking is made up of routine chores.

To be true artists we have to learn to live in the present. We need to learn from the past, act in the here and now, and prepare for future consequences. To live well in the present we need what modern people might call 'job satisfaction'. We need to feel that what we do is well done, creative, necessary and appreciated. If all these demands are met our soul expands and our sense of purpose deepens. We are truly nourished.

Devotion

Here is yet another old-fashioned word. We might assume that it means a religious act of prayer even more stringently applied than reverence. This is true, but it is far more than that. To be devoted means to give yourself entirely to the thing to which you are devoted. It means to perform every task with a loving attitude towards everything that exists, both within yourself and in the world around you.

If you devote yourself to what you are doing, you do it wholeheartedly. You are conscious of what you are doing, while also loving what you are doing. Devoting yourself to something implies that you have commitment to as well as love for the thing.

The extraordinary consequences of devotion are that you can do your duty without resentment. You learn to love your duty. And when you love what you have to do, then you are doing what you love to do!

Devotion brings with it an intimate knowledge of things. You get to know the real inner aspect of all that you do.

When you devote yourself to another person you get to know them better than you know yourself.

Devotion means paying attention to the smallest detail. If you practise this exercise, you gradually become more alert to the reality of a task and then, if something is left out or skimmed over, it begins to hurt. Every part of a chore asks to be done as properly and as beautifully as possible. Devotion is an attitude of soul.

As with all meditative exercises, I suggest beginning in small ways. Select a task you particularly like, or dislike, and do it with devotion. The reason that your feelings should be strongly engaged is that it will stimulate the artist in you.

You may, of course, begin more objectively and simply select a task that you find easy to perform. It will not only become more interesting, surprising you with hidden aspects, but it will also begin to suggest to you better ways of doing it. Eventually you will find an artistic expression inherent in the job that you never saw before. The outcome will be immense satisfaction, physically, mentally and spiritually.

If this is too demanding, try the following.

Stop, look, listen

When you have completed a task, stop, look at it and listen to what it is telling you. For example, when you have made the bed, cleaned the room and opened the window, stand still at the door and look at the beauty, order and cleanliness you have created. Listen to the space, to the sounds of the room, and be happy. Smell the clean smell and rejoice. Enjoy the colours, the movement of the light, the arrangements of objects, and maybe observe that the room would just need the finishing touch of a plant or a vase of flowers. Or maybe a picture needs straightening.

If you decide to do this on the completion of one task every day, you will begin to see how creative you are and how much more creative you could become.

The exercise does not ask you to linger and congratulate yourself, nor to linger and dwell on the imperfections. It asks you to enjoy, to correct where possible and to love the outcome of your work. Eventually, you will love the work itself, as an artist loves the labour that leads to artistic satisfaction.

Attention to detail

This is not as arduous as it sounds, nor will it take you away from the needs of daily life. Just pay attention to what you are doing as you do it. Notice what tools you are using. Observe whether they are working properly. Give your full attention to the task in hand. Try not to plan your next task while engaged in what you are doing. Only move on to the next task when you have completed the present one as well as possible.

Not only will you be much more satisfied with what you have done but will also find that you can do it quicker and with much greater efficiency, and that the end result is a job well done rather than half-done. The practice of this exercise stimulates your memory unconsciously, in that your movements will remember how to do things properly without you having to think about it. And you will enjoy the movements, their effects and the energy you save.

Wonder

This exercise really takes no time at all unless you choose to dwell on it. Decide to relish something every day. There will be no day that passes in which something wonderful does not happen. It may even be to wonder at something *not* happening! These are small miracles, too!

At first, in your moment of reflection, you may think you saw nothing wonderful that day. Never mind. Just decide to try again tomorrow. Gradually you will notice the remarkable wonders that make up our daily life.

Prayer

Homemaking is a challenge. It is both wonderful and terrible. We can rejoice and quail at the magnitude of the responsibilities. And we can at times feel very, very lonely.

In moments of stress it is not uncommon to turn to prayer. But when we feel happy and in control of our lives it is easy to forget that there are higher powers accompanying us also. Prayer, when in need, is very valid, and praying when *not* in need is just as valid. When we pray, we acknowledge our angel and enter into conversation with her.

Speech is a remarkable human faculty. No other creature can express itself as clearly, as imaginatively and as meaningfully as a human being. We use words all the time. And we hear words, understand their meaning and act upon them. We think in words much of the time, though we also think in pictures. Pictorial thinking stimulates and utilizes imagination. Word thinking stimulates and utilizes comprehension.

Prayer can really only be understood by starting to do it. And prayer almost always involves the word. We pray with words, saying them aloud or speaking silently in the heart. Of course, some prayers occur in pictorial images; these are the deep soul-prayers that we make to our angel quite unconsciously. Our very trust in the fact that tomorrow will be another day is a form of soul-prayer.

To pray deliberately requires a vehicle, and so we choose a verse or poem, a thought or a religious text. But unless it has meaning for us we cannot pray with it.

Find something that has meaning for you and suits you. You may need a variety of prayers, because prayer is usually related to a particular need, and needs vary. Offer your prayer either before you go to sleep or when you wake. At these moments of changing consciousness you are closest to your angel. You can therefore remember the relationship with your angel before going to sleep, and remember the fruits of the prayer much better on wakening.

It is not necessary to dwell intellectually on the words of the prayer. In fact, this can be counter-productive because angels do not understand the words themselves. They understand the *gesture* of the words. They receive the *soul picture* of the words.

Just as a work of art feeds the soul, so do soul pictures of words feed the angels. They receive the food we human beings send to them and return the gift by painting pictures of truth and reconciliation in us. These angelic pictures are food for us. It is not uncommon to be intellectually unaware of the new soul pictures. However, they inform our moods, our thinking and our actions and alter them so that they can be more creative and less selfish. Learning to become aware of the efficacy of prayer means that you are learning to listen to and understand the voice of your angel.

Prayers need not be complicated supplications. A prayer need only be sincere. It is best if the prayer is concluded with words already mentioned in previous chapters: *Not my will, but thy will be done.*

We are prone to hold onto things too long, to become embroiled in things, narrowing our options and closing the door on redemption. By saying the words above, you can give away the pain or problem to your angel, who surveys your real destiny, intentions and aims. By letting go, you allow another to help you see your real purpose once more. You are no longer alone.

Joy

Homemaking has many delightful and rich aspects. Festivals, mealtimes, birthdays, parties, visitors, all bring fresh content into the home. It is really quite easy to be creative, to be joyful at such moments. However, homemaking is largely the ordinary humdrum affairs of life, when joy can become muted or cease altogether.

Perhaps the key to understanding why we lose joy in life is to address the question of loneliness. Those moments when joy propels us are the times when we are together with others or spiritually satisfied with ourselves. We say that we are *enjoying* ourselves. To enjoy means that someone else joins me in the enjoyment or I feel completely at peace with myself.

Joy is self-engendered. It comes from the heart and soul and invites others to join me in my joy. Remember that we are *always* accompanied by an angel, a spirit being whose task it is to assist us in walking along our chosen path in life. We are never alone. Once we trust in our angel, our angel can be heard by us. That we do not hear her is not her fault.

Joy is the result of hearing the angel. A radiant light shines up in the soul. Being in the presence of someone who lives their life with joy is most enjoyable. Joy stimulates creativity, and being creative engenders joy.

5

Validating Feeling

Secreting

The physical body is a marvellous piece of workmanship.
Hidden within it are all manner of different substances,
working together in harmony, bringing health so that the
soul and spirit can function. Processing alien substances, such
as food, is the job of the *life process of secreting*. It sorts out what
is nutritious from what is poisonous, absorbs the good and
excretes the rest. The mystery this involves is implicit in the
very word; we know very little about it and how it actually
works. We are hardly conscious of its activity. It is a well kept
secret but when it does not do its job, we are all too aware of
the problem and fall ill. It is our immune system, our pro-

tection against what might harm us, as well as the digester and transformer of everything that enters us.

In the physical body the process is one of digesting, in the ether body of transforming, and in the soul it is the power of feeling. The ego can understand and deal with daily life because the soul digests impressions, and sorts through them so that they can be thought about and acted upon. We say we have a feeling for things or that something does not feel right. Some people act upon their feelings, and some people prefer to digest information before acting upon it.

Unfortunately, we do not really trust our feelings. We are led to believe that thinking is a much safer and more accurate faculty for decision-making than feeling. In point of fact, neither one is better than the other. They are quite simply different powers. The one is directed from the head, the other flows from the heart. Thinking imaginatively is like the light of the sun, feeling from the heart is like sun-warmed, life-giving water.

It is assumed by most people that parenting, homemaking and housekeeping is something everyone just knows how to do. There is no need to learn anything about it before embarking, and anyway we all have our different ways, our different standards, our different outlooks. Homemakers find it hard to accept being told what to do by outside agencies. We intensely object to the 'nanny culture' of our time, feeling it as interference and infringement of freedom and rights. My home is my castle.

And yet sometimes we realize that we have lost or squandered the funds to keep up the castle. Things can get beyond our control. We discover that we can no longer rely on the riches of our instincts to protect and keep us safe from harm. And feeling, as already discussed, has been put out to grass.

Even when we know that too much television may be damaging, we can find ourselves giving in to external pressure. Even when we know that a set time for bed may be very healthy, we can find ourselves unable to establish it. Even when we know that regular mealtimes are essential, we can find ourselves pushed about by life's demands, allowing meals to become random events taken on the trot.

From where does this 'knowing' come? Is it something on which we can rely? It has taken millennia for human beings to develop the faculty of thinking. In olden times people felt about things rather than thought about them. They saw living spirits behind every material object; and when we look at artefacts of old we are astonished at their beauty. Nothing was merely functional. Everything was decorated, often with scenes depicting its use, and imbued with feeling as a recognized and valued faculty.

Feeling for things is not quite the same thing as instinct. Our healthy instincts are there for us to use as a safeguard against harm. However, today we seem to have lost or watered down this faculty too. We no longer trust our instincts, or seem not to be in touch with them. Because we have so sharpened our faculty of thinking, we can no longer expect our instincts to be as alert as they were in the past.

Instinct

It is not uncommon to hear a 'still, small voice' within us that tells us what to do at moments of indecision. For some people this voice is utterly reliable. It is what we call gut instinct, and very often listening to it saves us a huge amount of bother.

But it is also possible that the inner voice is sometimes wrong or not appropriate to the occasion. Our instincts will always speak up to protect our body from harm. Instinct relates entirely to our physical existence. Sometimes we need to listen to our soul intuitions rather than our instincts, which invariably work in the interest of self-preservation. However, we know very well that sometimes the preservation of someone else is more important than our own safety, demonstrated, for instance, by a mother's instinct to protect her child before herself. The human soul has very little that can safeguard it from harm. The astral body contains our emotions, thinking, feeling and motivation. It is directed by sympathy and antipathy, which respond to others' emotional life or astrality by connecting with their moods and ideas, and sensing their emotions. We can easily recognize this by imagining being with someone who is angry. We get caught in their negativity unless we do something to defend ourselves against their mood. Of course, the same may be true when someone is happy—we get caught up in their infectious positivity.

Equally, we can easily find ourselves tuning in to what someone else is thinking, and do what someone else is doing. This can be very positive. It is the method parents employ to help their children do what they need to do. There is no better teacher than a good example. And imitation is a very positive instinct.

However, the example we set also derives from the emotions we display, and so whether we are a good or bad role model can depend on our mood. In this context, children's imitation extends to reproducing the moods and feelings displayed. Because we are often the primary role model at home, it would be nice to be able to direct everyone to the good!

Whilst instinct derives from the bodily functions of secreting via our glandular and lymph system, the still small voice that we hear, which comes to us from the heart, is that of intuition. It is our angel speaking to us, quietly showing us what the best reaction to a person or event might be. This quiet voice is not pushy and not protective. To hear this voice clearly we need to trust our feelings. Feelings and emotions are not identical. Emotions are feelings filled with passions, with loves and hates, often directed by our bodily functions. The faculty of feeling in contrast is our ability to flow, like the waters of life, in and out of the soul of the world or the soul of another person.

There are two kinds of knowledge. One is wisdom knowledge that reflects the wisdom of angels. We see this knowledge working sublimely in small children as well as in old people, who know so much from life experience. The other is intellectual knowledge, clear, logical, rational thinking. This is the knowledge modern people believe to be the best and most objective.

However, neither is really better or more objective than the other. Both are equally valid. The best thing is, if possible, to feel deeply into our wisdom knowledge, use our intellect to shed light on this wisdom and then, with love, embark on consequent actions. Homemaking is a task at the cutting edge of this new path, and homemakers can pave the way for a more loving thinking which has, nevertheless, not lost its clarity but validates feeling as a legitimate faculty.

Thinking alone will never tell us anything about a person's inner aims. Feeling will lead us gently towards an understanding, which we can then think about. Gut instinct still works but is perhaps too self-orientated. *Intuition* is the new instinct born out of love. We do not have to protect ourselves. We can trust that the other is working towards love, just as we are. However, to rely upon intuition it is necessary first to find self-control. Intuition cannot be heard clearly when emotions are flying about or instinct is gathering for self-protection. For wisdom knowledge to speak we need to be silent.

We make many mistakes because we believe we cannot trust our feelings. The ego is as much engaged in feeling the world as it is in thinking about the world. However, the information comes to us by different means, through the heart or the head. We have only one central organ, the heart. We can be brain dead and still be alive. We cannot be heart dead and still live. Those who trust their feelings alongside their thinking will be well on the way to a new intuition based on self-control.

Self-control

Homemaking is a vocation, and a vocation implies making a sacrifice. The word itself implies that we are 'called' to the task rather than just pursuing a career. This can often lead, though, to a sense of not being in control of life, events and, most of all, our own needs. We can feel as if our soul is stretched out so thin that anything will cause us to snap. We see all that needs to be done and cannot find the wherewithal to do it. Life just simply takes over and chaos ensues.

Then there are days when we get up ready for the fray, determined to take charge and, instead of confrontation and challenge, everything flows beautifully. There can also be days when we take a stand, directing everything like a military campaign. The result may be very satisfactory in terms of efficiency, but we may feel very left out of other people's love.

Self-control does not mean taking charge and leading from the front, even though we may be quite within our rights to do this. Instead it means to listen quietly and peacefully to our own still, small voice of intuition and then act accordingly, whilst being fully aware of all the other people around us.

As we have seen, this voice of intuition lives in the heart. It starts to speak when we allow our feelings to 'digest' events and people. Tact is one of the results of this. Another is empathy. Yet another, perhaps the most essential, is being in the right place at the right time.

Emotions come into play when feelings get out of hand and thought no longer plays its disciplined part. Emotions are like naughty children. They need a stern word and a firm hand to keep them under control. It helps to bring our thinking into the picture, to shed clear light upon the emotions, and then true feeling can arise, filled with wisdom knowledge. Whenever we get emotional, something real and true lies beneath. But unless we silence the emotions so that our true feelings can be heard, thinking cannot shed its light. The wonderful thing about the astral body is that through it we share everything in common with every other human being. We recognize strengths and weaknesses only because we share those strengths and weaknesses. This is an excellent starting point for developing self-control.

Meditative exercises for secreting and instinct

The homemaker is the person who makes the home. She is the focus of needs, the organizer, and often the person who carries out the tasks. No one can perform adequately and effectively unless in control of the self. To be able to make a decision and act upon it requires understanding a need, and recognizing the right action to take in response. For this to happen fruitfully, we need to be centred and controlled. This means taking charge of our moods and emotions, which are a large part of our astral body.

Shared strengths make us stronger—so much so that we may begin to imagine that they are ours alone and take all the credit! Stepping into the space where we can clearly hear our inner voice helps us to weed out what requires weeding, and to cultivate that which needs cultivating.

Humility

This old-fashioned virtue has lost some of its true meaning. We take it to mean making ourselves less than another. To the homemaker, this idea is not a pleasant one because all too often she feels the lesser in any case!

Humility actually implies much more than being humble. It implies acknowledging your imperfections. In the moment that you do this you have two choices: to bow down under the weight of them, or to take them up as a challenge to be overcome. You will, unfortunately, not make any step towards perfection without identifying your imperfections.

Don't be afraid. We are all imperfect. To have the courage to own up to your imperfections is immensely stimulating. Remind yourself how much courage it takes to exercise humility. Do this every morning. Use courage as the new transformed humility that can bravely take on difficulties and then, with warmth of heart, begin to overcome them.

Oddly enough, once an imperfection is recognized and taken on board, a feeling of strength and freedom enters the soul. Your angel receives humility and returns it as soul-pictures bearing in them the means to overcome the imperfection. The still small voice of true feeling will tell you what to do and how to do it. You will, with humility, move steadily and purposefully towards self-control.

The practice is as follows:

The moment you realize you have made a mistake or are wrong, acknowledge it.

Apologize immediately.

If an explanation is required, ask for time to do this *later*.

Take as long as you need to 'digest' the event.

When you 'feel' the time is right, calmly explain.

It is quite possible that you will begin to experience moments when *only you* notice your errors. Follow the above practice silently. The apology is given to your angel.

Practising humility in this structured way opens up potential for real and courageous self-control. It is of particular importance to practise this exercise if you are interacting with children. Their souls absorb your courage, which encourages their dawning self-control.

Honesty

This may not seem very hard to practise. But you will surprise yourself by how often you excuse yourself or tell yourself little white lies. Do not make the mistake of thinking that being honest with yourself is easier than being honest with another. It is just as difficult.

Decide, upon awakening, to be honest at least once today. It is helpful to take a moment in the middle of the day to assess yourself with regard to honesty. It is easier to be honest in the broad light of day. However, you can take yourself awfully seriously and bring out the whip over small infractions of truth. We all make mistakes. Forgiveness is essential, also forgiveness of yourself.

Self-assessing without the fierce scrutiny of honesty is not very refreshing. But self-assessing without the balm of forgiveness is debilitating.

Honesty embraces all and everything. Also the ability to laugh at yourself. Laughter, even a rueful smile, puts things into perspective.

Humour

A sense of humour cannot be invented. Moreover, it cannot be quantified or qualified. It is an entirely personal faculty. However, we all know what taking ourselves too seriously can do.

Try to find one moment in the day that made you smile or even laugh at yourself. Enjoy it and relive it. It is very refreshing. A sense of the ridiculous is a quality to cultivate. Humour helps us to see ourselves from the outside as an observer would do.

Observation

Every situation that you meet, every person you encounter, has a gift to offer. However, in order to get to know what this gift might be, you need to become very observant.

Before going to sleep, remember an encounter that perhaps you dealt with badly or that made you uncomfortable after it had passed. Try to discover what you were feeling at the time.

Let the feeling rise to your awareness and then let it go.

On the following day, revisit the scene. The feeling will begin to tell you something important, either about yourself or about the situation.

On the following day, the new, important view will make sense and you will know what you have learnt.

Observation is a slow and delicate exercise. However, there is no hurry. Life is a great teacher and takes her time. You may find that at first nothing changes. Persevere, because things will be changing around you. Those who live with you will experience that your reactions are far less emotional and very much more filled with true feeling.

Point and circle meditation

Finding your centre, your true, effective self, is the key to managing life in the home. Here the ego needs to take charge. However, the ego by itself can become egotistical and make things work to serve its own ends. In order to work selflessly yet decisively, the following meditative exercise is very helpful.

In the evening before you go to sleep, remember the words: *In me is God*. Then picture a bright shining circle of light with a blue centre point.

In the morning, upon awakening, remember the words: *I am in God*. Then picture to yourself a blue circle around a bright point of light.

These are one and the same picture, the one filling your ego with the light of God, the other radiating the light back to God.

You may not be happy with the word 'God'. It doesn't matter. The bright shining light that I call 'God' may have another name for you. Use the name that for you has the meaning of spirit-filled creator being.

The ego in its purity is a spirit-filled creator being *in its infancy*. Just as a baby contains the potential to be a self-directing free human being, so does each ego bear the potential to be a creator being.

The meditative exercise helps us to learn this startling truth and to accept it humbly.

Intuition

To accept the full responsibility of homemaking can be terrifying. Even if we know we are not alone but can rely upon our angel, as well as the other members of our house community, we always know that the buck stops with us in the end. No one can be all-wise and all-knowing all the time. Mistakes will and do happen.

The moment we accept this with humility, honesty and a strong dose of humour, our emotions relax their stranglehold on our real being and allow us to become more active in our feeling. As soon as the ego begins to work in the astral body, feelings can be drawn up into the light of thinking to be used properly, in the right place at the right time. This is intuition. We can trust our intuition and not leave things to instinct alone. We can work from our own centre, confident that we will know what to do and will be where we should be, when we need to be.

Honesty and humility help to awaken the golden potential in the ego and provide the courage we need to trust our feelings. We need no longer fear our untamed emotions. We can be confident that wisdom knowledge and intellectual knowledge are working smoothly together in the soul and in the ego. The ego can become like the sun that shines warmly and brightly over the world.

6
Establishing Vitality

Everyday things that sap vitality

Feeling resentful; overriding others; putting efficiency before all; clockwatching; having the tendency to blame others; being controlling; feeling over-responsible; tendency to intolerance; making snap decisions; not good at taking on board the views of others; tendency to nag; inclined to favouritism; easily upset at changes of routine; unreasonably sticking to one's guns; easily ashamed; upset when plans don't work out; nursing grudges.

Maintaining

Maintaining the home involves continuous activity. However, not all of us like this aspect of the task. To some it is rewarding and satisfying because everyday chores, the routines of life, can be the backbone of sanity. Many people turn to basic household tasks as a means of clearing the head, finding such mundane activities refreshing. When mental stress becomes too much, the simplicity of scrubbing or baking or cooking can be a relief. To others it is mind-numbingly tedious. Each day seems to bring the same tasks; cleaning, cooking, shopping, school runs, laundry, just seem to repeat themselves endlessly. A doctor's visit may feel like a delightful break in the monotony!

However, the *process of maintaining* life in our bodies is anything but boring. We know the awful feeling when we are unwell, lacking in life and energy. Exactly how the body maintains itself is a great secret. It happens somewhere in a hidden part of our being and usually we are only aware of the process when it is not working very well, in other words, when we fall ill. When we are well we are almost unaware of our physical body. It functions smoothly, doing whatever we ask it to. The same goes for our soul. We can feel light and easy, and solid and real, our emotions responding and reacting to inner and outer stimuli with humour and empathy. But when we fail to maintain our personal needs, our personal space, we can dry out, get frustrated, blocked up inside and closed off to the world. I believe that homemakers are particularly prone to using up their inner resources, neglecting to replenish and revitalize their soul. Perhaps this particular weakness stems from the reality of trying to serve the greater needs of others. However, if we are to answer the needs of others effectively we cannot afford to ignore our own needs. We are morally obliged to maintain ourselves too.

Maintaining the physical body is centred in our cellular regeneration in the marrow of our bones. Right at the centre of the hardest part of the body lies the core of life, the place where our immune system originates. Our life body generates itself in a constant activity of renewal in its own image. Though I may change as I get older, the principle of who I am makes me real for the whole of my lifespan on earth, thus maintaining me.

In the soul there is a constant activity of replenishment too. Smaller and bigger impressions continue to work through memories, repeatedly recurring. The soul draws up memories according to outer and inner needs and stimuli. We add to our store of them as time goes by.

Of course, in our daily, humdrum lives we are usually unaware that we are living out our karma. (Karma is the self-chosen destiny which we bring with us from a pre-birth existence into life, with the tasks and learning challenges particular to ourselves.) We are unaware that little things need maintaining in order that the bigger things can be sustained. This is probably a good thing, because if we were constantly aware of the fact that our every little action is making a difference to our own as well as other people's lives we might feel like the centipede who could not decide which of her hundred legs to put forward first and so did nothing for the rest of her life! Some part of us, luckily, recognizes that if the home is well maintained and rhythms, routines and cleanliness are upheld, we are happier and healthier. So we do the daily chores, sometimes cheerfully, often begrudgingly, and we long for something called freedom from care and an endless source of energy with which to enjoy it.

On the days when our energy level is good, our mood is positive and the weather is fine, we can zip through the chores and find time to do a great number of other things besides. But there are those terrible days when it all seems to get out of hand and we lack the energy to pull ourselves together. Revitalizing ourselves by finding time for recreational activity is high up on the list of things we prize.

We may decide to set aside a part of our day for ourselves, to think, read, run or whatever we find restores our inner and outer balance. But then a smaller or bigger crisis occurs and the first thing to be sacrificed is that precious space we have carved out of our busy lives for what we consider to be selfish reasons. It goes without saying that it would be quite impossible to maintain those personal moments at the cost of our children. It would, moreover, possibly be counter-productive. Parents know only too well that switching off from the children only seems to make them more and more demanding. So what is the key to unlocking the secret chamber where we maintain and vitalize ourselves, in order to re-establish our necessary energy levels?

Drive

Deep within the human soul lies a faculty that can save us from running ourselves into the ground. Psychologists call it 'drive'. We can see ourselves as the driver of a car, fully in control and going places of our own choice, stopping and starting at will along a road we know, towards a place we wish to reach.

Our subconscious self in its wisdom knowledge knows what our body needs in order to survive. We experience healthy drive when we know hunger, thirst, pain and other basic sensations. We used to know what was dangerous to us and flee from it, just as we knew what was good for us and were drawn to it. The human being of today still has drives, but our intellectual knowledge has overridden our wisdom knowledge and we can deny our own inner self-knowledge and make free decisions, even doing what may be harmful to us.

Nowadays I believe we can describe a transformed drive for survival as the voice of conscience. It is the voice of human wisdom knowledge filled with the vitality of our guardian angel. And when we listen to it, the outcome is often surprisingly positive, turning potentially destructive things into welcome developments. Our conscience tells us where we go wrong, but it also tells us where we can go right.

It is a great shame that we listen to it more often when we are being warned away than when we are being encouraged to go forward. If our conscience can save us from doing wrong, why should it not be equally valuable when it tells us to be proactive?

By listening to our conscience we can discover a self that can be both effective and sensitive. We discover that it may well be worthwhile to take a little time out of the day for something recreational and that this need not mean selfishly stealing from the greater good, but rather a necessary sustaining of vitality—not only for survival, as our drive tells us, but also for creative living, which our conscience dictates. In fact there is such a thing as healthy selfishness. It is just as imperative to refresh the self as it is necessary to eat, drink and sleep.

The odd thing about human beings is that we tend to focus on our faults rather than our inventive and imaginative aspects. Of course, we all have faults. Our astral body by itself, without direction from the ego, is certainly a creature of passions, anger, hate, greed and lust. But it is also endowed with faith, love, hope, goodness, peace, contentment, creativity. By curbing the astral body's negative aspects, the inner self can transform these into virtues.

Self-sacrifice, a most excellent virtue, may be necessary at times but is it useful to the point of martyrdom? Martyrdom can be a very difficult thing for the other people with whom we live. It can make them feel guilty, possibly even paralysing their helpfulness. Renewal of the self for the sake of having time and energy for others is not selfish. It is merely sensible. However, we need self-confidence to listen to our conscience. We also need to create time to work constructively with the wisdom knowledge we know as the drive towards health and vitality.

Self-confidence

Being self-confident depends on us knowing our own strengths and weaknesses, and working with them in full trust that we are following our conscience within the environment in which we are active. Bashing ahead, confident that something or other will bale us out when the going gets tough is not a sustainable form of self-confidence. Keeping everything under a tight rein of control is also not the most enlivening form of self-confidence. In fact, it is often extremely exhausting. Maintaining routine against all odds usually makes everyone in the home very uncomfortable and sometimes even rebellious. It is simply impossible to control every event and quite impossible to control other people without doing considerable damage to all parties involved.

To keep a routine running yet allow for surprises and upsets as well as keep our sanity, and find time for ourselves in a constantly changing environment, requires a great deal of skilful self-confidence. We are like jugglers keeping all the balls in the air at once. We call this the art of 'multi-tasking'. At the centre of it all—unless the task is shared—stands one single person, alone in her work yet in constant contact with many others, who move in and out, each doing their bit to keep the home running smoothly. Without self-confidence, the balls keep dropping. The energy required to pick one up whilst keeping three others going is tremendous. Usually the first ball to be dropped is time for ourselves. We let it go as the most expendable. In effect, we are declaring ourselves to be the least important aspect of the home when actually we are the hub of the wheel.

Without faith and trust in ourselves as a vital organ of spiritual, social and practical use, we become control freaks. How can we have faith and confidence in others if we have no faith in ourselves?

Being methodical and tidy, and sticking to routines are indeed great energy savers. In times of stress we can gratefully recognize this. Tidy clothes cupboards save time in the mornings. Replacing food in the larder means we always have something to cook. Secure in the well-oiled routine of everyday life, we find energy and freedom.

However, we use up a great deal of our life forces thinking and planning. Trying to cook a meal in someone else's kitchen demonstrates this. It can take twice the time we would need in our own kitchen. The more we know our environment, the more self-confidence grows. Self-confidence flourishes when the ground under our feet is solid and stable. We can allow ourselves the time to reconnect with the self and tune in to our conscience in peace and harmony.

A good negative comparison might be an earthquake. We lose our centre of gravity because the normally steady and solid ground beneath our feet suddenly moves, shaking our inner and outer confidence. Self-confidence based on self-knowledge is an unshakeable inner foundation that makes us feel in tune with destiny and thus free to tune in to those with whom we share the home.

Controlling our environment can create a false sense of self-confidence. We know we are in charge of maintaining the home and therefore may sometimes claim the right to control everything that happens in the home. With regard to the daily routines and chores, to the organization and administration, we are quite justified in taking control. We may even justifiably expect certain things to be done in a certain way, especially if we are bringing up children. This is obviously best done by setting a good example, though there may be times when we actually have to demand certain standards. However, if this leads to controlling the way in which others express themselves, then we are in trouble. The pseudo self-confidence of the 'control freak' has superseded real self-confidence. By attempting to control everything and everyone, no matter how subtly, we expend an enormous amount of energy and time second-guessing and manipulating. We can eventually grow to dislike ourselves, another exhausting and deadening experience.

By turning our attention to the humble life process of maintaining, however, we can appreciate how it keeps on renewing the body. It revitalizes our whole being quietly and successfully, confidently and effectively, throughout our lives. In the soul, the force we know as the drive wakens us up to what is and is not physically healthy or good for us. And as long as we listen to our drive, our body will maintain good health. The voice of conscience keeps us walking on the path of our destiny, interacting with the destinies of others. Self-confidence, or in other words faith in oneself, is maintained by learning to listen to our conscience and trusting in it as implicitly as we trust in our angel.

Meditative exercises for maintaining vitality and drive

Maintaining vitality as an exercise is a form of self-discipline. To ease our way into this unfashionable idea we can use the faithful servants of our routines. Establishing good habits is essential. We are free to alter them to suit the occasion and even to abandon them should they become obsolete. We can create new habits or vary them if we are confident that they are appropriate. To have the self-confidence to change our life patterns requires a sense of being at home with our real inner self. Exercising self-discipline is a safe way to discover our potential.

To stay in control without controlling everything, to feel in charge of our destiny without denying the same freedom to others, to repeat chores day after day without becoming bored and resentful, and to build trust and faith in self and others are exciting and worthwhile challenges. As with all high expectations, it is best to start simply, taking everything step by step.

Forgiveness

To forgive is something about which our conscience speaks loudly and clearly. It can seem quite easy to forgive and we usually tag onto it the concept of forgetting. To forgive is easy when you also forget. But perhaps our forgetting takes pride of place over forgiveness.

Forgiving includes understanding the perpetrator of the slight and how and why the insult was delivered. And it includes yourself, and how and why the action was received as an insult.

To forgive, therefore, must include *remembering* the event correctly. It is necessary to sort out what aspect belongs to the apparent perpetrator and what aspect to the recipient. In every event that requires forgiveness, two are implicated.

If an insult or hurt is perceived, first try to remember the
event in its correct sequence.
Then sort out why it happened.
Next, sort out how it happened.
Then accept responsibility for your part in the event.
Then let go of what belongs to the other person in the
event.
Next, apologize for your part in the event.
Finally, do not expect to receive an apology from the other
person.

Though this may seem a very cumbersome and lengthy
exercise, it is in fact quite simple to follow. You can be doing
some ordinary chore in your daily routine whilst sorting out a
perceived slight or even a very deep hurt. In fact, I would
recommend practising active forgiveness whilst doing
mindless chores. The regularity of the body's movement
soothes the wounded soul and assists memory.

The hard part is apologizing. It is wonderful when the
apology is received but you can feel a second pain if you are
rebuffed. However, remember that you have learned from
your part in the affair. You cannot control the other's part nor
how she decides to deal with it. Bearing a grudge or hanging
on to a slight is possibly the most debilitating experience.
Perhaps only jealousy ranks higher. Forgiveness releases vital
energy, which can be used to build reliable self-confidence.

Waiting

This exercise can be a stepping stone towards practising
forgiveness. It merely requires allowing spaces to exist
between events. We have an unfortunate tendency to get

impatient with gaps that are unprepared or unexpected, and thus feel we are wasting time. Active waiting means to let the gaps become peace-filled moments of non–activity. Out of such precious moments deep insights can arise. Waiting actively means learning to be alone and at peace with yourself.

As a consequence, it becomes less and less necessary to control life or manipulate situations. Waiting actively awakens the knowledge that what should come towards you will come, and you do not need to rush out to meet it.

Steadfastness

Here is another old-fashioned word, implying steadiness and faithfulness. Life is filled with the need to make decisions. They can be big or small, but no matter what the size or seriousness, we always feel good if we decide for ourselves. Then life takes over and we can find ourselves vacillating, reconsidering, seeking advice and moving restlessly between all the better ideas that flow towards us. When we exercise steadfastness, we arrive at inner peace.

First make your decision.
Keep to it resolutely until a new recognition makes you question it.
Make your new decision.
Keep to it until greater wisdom makes you question it.
And so on.

Steadfastness is anything but paralysing. By practising this exercise you will discover new wisdom and certainty as well as strengthening self-confidence.

Appreciation

We live, work with and interact with others our whole lives. We get to know ourselves because others reflect us back to ourselves. It is often only because of how others react to us that we discover that what we may have intended as a good deed turns out to have actually been a very bad idea! To practise appreciation requires very little effort on our part but has a very strong reverberating effect.

First, take note of what others do.
Focus on what is good and helpful.
Thank them.
Make this a daily practice and personalize it for every member with whom you live.
Start by appreciating one thing in each person every day. In time it will grow to an all-round appreciation of life itself. You will get to know yourself ever better. And good energy will stir in you. A wonderful spin-off from this exercise is that you will begin to notice that others appreciate you! Remember to receive this graciously.

The pedagogical law

The following exercise requires daily self-assessment. This must be done alone and in peace and quiet. It is best done in the morning before others get up, or in the evening before going to bed. It is a specific method that is essential especially in relation to situations that seem to sap all your energy and strength. It is based on the fact that a human being is constituted of four aspects or 'bodies', each of which have a definite function and which, when combined, make you the decisive, thinking, feeling, living, physical being who can make things happen and be effective in the world.

Your ego, the primary director and deepest self, is the highest principle with which you can work. Next comes your soul, a body of emotions, thinking, feeling and actions. Still lower yet permeating all with vitality is your life body. Lower than all, but also indispensable for making your mark in life on earth, is your physical body, the house in which the other three dwell. There can be no question that your ego is in charge of all. If your ego takes charge, your soul is brought under your control, thereby freeing your life forces to motivate and energize your body. Then you can do what you really want to do in life. You are no longer a prey to your emotions, your likes and dislikes, your loves and fears.

If you are in charge of your astral body, your energy and vitality will no longer be sapped by your inner failures, and your physical body can be revitalized by your life body.

The effect on others with whom you live can be subtle or startling. It is true to say that your moods not only sap your energy, but they sap and sway the energy of others. If you are in control of yourself, others can flourish. Moreover, others will probably feel stimulated to follow your example and take charge of their own emotional soul or astrality. You will not need to tell them.

The exercise takes the burden of negative astrality out of the equation and clears the way for your ether body to refresh itself; in turn this strengthens the life bodies of those with whom you interact.

Start by assessing who is in charge of you, or what is driving you.

Having decided that you are in charge of yourself, take a moment to assess how you are projecting towards others.

Make a new decision to control your emotions, so that you only project those you choose to project, and that are appropriate to the occasion.

Allow the others space and freedom to do the same.

Then proceed with your tasks.

As always, start simply. If someone is shouting and you feel you may be getting involved, decide to answer in a soft voice, perhaps even by whispering. If someone is demanding or dictating unpleasantly, decide to do what you deem reasonable and not undertake what is unreasonable. Refrain from arguing with the other person about it. Just do it quietly and cheerfully. If others refuse to do what needs to be done, quietly set them an example by doing what needs to be done yourself.

As with all meditative exercises, the trick is to start. Success eventually comes with practice. Remember to forgive yourself for your failings, and above all remember to start again, every day.

Tranquillity

Home life is often a hive of activity, especially when everyone who lives there is at home. Equally often, everyone except the homemaker is out about their business, and the house is empty. However, empty and tranquil are not synonymous. To be tranquil is to be at peace with the world and all that is in it. It is to have faith and hope in life's goodness. Founded on your own inner striving to bring goodness, truth and peace into your own life, you can begin to spread tranquillity around you. Steadfastness, forgiveness, appreciation and creative control of your negative astrality all contribute to enlivening energy and health. Then peace enfolds life. You are on the way to transforming impatience into waiting actively for the wisdom of your own conscience to direct you on the path of destiny.

7
Developing Insight

Growing

Wouldn't it be wonderful if we knew everything? If we knew the reasons for things, why they happened and where they were taking us? If we knew the secrets of life, knew all there is to know about the universe and why we exist at all? Most people feel they are on a path of discovery. There are, of course, moments when we think we have arrived, but usually we quickly realize that whole realms still wait to be explored. Human beings never cease to grow, move forward, develop. Most of all, our soul faculties expand and grow through every life experience, through every joy and sorrow. Often, it is the painful experiences that teach us the most, though great happiness and contentment can also be the basis for new knowledge and unexpected wisdom.

Developing insight, real knowledge and understanding of what life is all about can come quite naturally to some people. To others, it is a process of trial and error. For yet others it involves the conscious decision to make connections between events, people and experiences.

We stand at the centre of life in the home, but it is not uncommon to experience this as being on the margins of life, sometimes even shut out from it. I urge everyone to undergo this apparently negative experience, for it is, in fact, the beginning of insight.

To see and understand a thing, you cannot always be right at the heart of it. You must be able to identify with its heart, whilst at the same time observing dispassionately how the heart beats and for what reason and purpose it pulsates. Real insight is to know all there is to know about a thing, from both inside and out.

It helps to be able to assess what went before and foresee what the future holds. We sometimes achieve this quite naturally by remembering the past and making an educated guess about a future outcome. However, insight is not something that happens because we are good at logic or can calculate cause and affect. It is a living quality of the heart and soul, of thinking and feeling working together on knowledge gained by true and accurate observation of facts. All too often we make quick assumptions about the random nature of facts that appear to have been the cause of an event. However, if these facts are properly examined they show themselves to be only external manifestations. To achieve knowledge of invisible spiritual facts means developing insight through an ever-growing, deepening knowledge of the human being.

The *life process of growing* in the physical body reaches a stage of completion. The process of soul growth or development, in contrast, is always active. The true self, the ego, gradually descends through the process of incarnation. The ego has infinite spiritual wisdom. That children often come out with wise and true statements is because their ego is hardly incarnated yet and still resides in the world of angels. They can say astonishing truths beyond the scope of adults, who have infinitely more life experience but often, sadly, infinitely less wisdom!

Many adults know that somewhere along the path to adulthood they have lost something. The desire to regain the innocent wisdom of childhood enlightened by conscious knowledge is a very healthy aim. Unhappiness easily stems from the realization that it is difficult to find time or space for our own self-development alongside a very busy daily schedule.

Desire

Desire is a faculty of the soul that leads towards the future. One can satisfy every desire and yet still desire more—there is something insatiable about it. This can make us shy away from it, identifying it as selfish and soul-destroying.

Of course, if we indulge desire for our own ends with no consideration of others at all it can certainly be selfish. Yet desire is alive in us and helps us to go forward, to grow and to want to achieve more. We talk about ambition as being selfish, but we also talk about healthy ambition.

Unfortunately, we equate desire and ambition with worldly things, an unsatisfiable longing for acquisitions, property, love life, pleasures of the flesh. Sad how easily we forget the multitude of good, true and purposeful things to be sought and won. Contentment is a virtue, for instance, which makes us pleasant to be with. Desire to further our inner growth, knowledge and wisdom makes us more interesting and rewarding for others.

Since humanity is far from perfect, there is great purpose in self-development. But we have to ask for whose sake we wish to develop. Simply to perfect ourselves without connecting with others and the world is certainly questionable. But the desire to grow inwardly as a means to help others can never be wrong. To do our work unhappily and with resentment because we don't accept our situation does not make a happy home for anyone.

Desire's mission is to help us progress. Suppressing it will only make it emerge negatively, so that we become restless and bitter about everything. Using innate desire to change and grow is infinitely fulfilling, especially if you have found a way that you can follow with a clear conscience.

Self-development

Self-development can be acquired in many different ways. Learning alongside your children, refreshing your education, taking up a specific study, or learning a new and exciting craft or instrument are all examples. But your path of growth can also involve learning to be content with ordinary household chores, to see virtue in life's daily activities.

Self-development is also an inner path. Because we cannot avoid interaction with others, we invariably encounter our own shortcomings. Although this is a very common experience, it is rarer to accept the challenge to change. It can be quite overwhelming to discover our personal deficiencies. Different people react differently to this awakening moment. Usually it will keep recurring, together with a realization that external ways of dealing with things are not enough. However, to embark on changing yourself can be daunting. It is not easy to alter old habits, especially habits of thought and feeling. Altering habitual actions is by far the easiest.

I could have lumped together all the meditative exercises in this book under the 'self-development' heading, but I separated them out because they offer different forms of help connected with each of the life processes. Common to all of them is the desire of the person practising them to seek some means of inner growth and change.

Questions often stand as a point of departure. The desire to know *why* is the beginning of wisdom and conscious knowledge. Nothing in the world would have been invented without human curiosity, the desire to explore, experiment and discover answers.

Today we can apply this same curiosity to the inner self. But it is hard to alter ourselves inwardly. No one else can do it for us. People can advise, cajole, persuade or educate us. But in the end we have to desire the change ourselves for it to have a lasting effect.

Resistance to change is very common. Change means uncertainty, newness. Some people leap into cold water with joy and delight, others need to dip in a toe, only gradually immersing themselves. Both ways eventually have a refreshing effect.

Self-development can only come about by overcoming resistance to change, by opening heart and mind to possibilities, by asking questions and desiring to find answers.

Curiosity is the result of desire rising to conscious thought. Then we can embark on the path of developing insight.

Meditative exercises for growing and desire

The first step in satisfying curiosity is to know that questions have answers. Yet the search for answers, the journey of discovery itself, is often far more educative than the actual conclusion. Along the way many varied and interesting developments surface, all of which contain new questions. So as not to get lost and distracted, we need some signposts on our chosen path.

Silence

When some occurrence gives rise to a question, our normal reaction is to begin to explore it either in thoughts, conversation or actions. However this can often drive the real question you should be asking underground, engendering inner restlessness.

Decide to be silent.
Let the question resound inwardly.
Let it live in your mind or heart as a question, without trying to find the answer.
Allow and welcome all the time it may take until the answer presents itself as a gift.
Let the answer arise.

The extraordinary thing about this exercise is that it can take days to find the answer or it can come in a flash of insight. The trick is to withhold your instantaneous reaction to a thing or person, allowing the healing balm of patient silence to fill you.

Working with your angel

Once you decide to embark on a path of self-development it is common to find that an important, meaningful book apparently falls off the bookshelf into your hand. Or you meet someone who can help you to begin. Or a window of opportunity just happens to open up.

These are not insignificant or chance events but the result of an unconscious collaboration between you and your angel. Your angel starts helping you, but you experience it as if coming from outside you. In reality your deeper self is beginning to talk to your angel.

The first step is to recognize this as significant and true, not coincidence.

In the morning on awakening, strive to remember the conversations you had with your angel during the night. These do not always come with words. They may come in pictures. They may come in moods. They may come in thoughts or colours. Let them live with you through the day.

The second step is to return your day's thoughts, feelings and moods to your angel before you go to sleep. Offer them up, without judging whether they were bad or good. Especially offer your most essential questions.

The lovely thing about this exercise is that it will not take long before you know what to do, and when and how to do it. At first it will feel as if you are being told how to deal with or relate to people, and you may wonder where such wisdom came from.

The third step is to trust in your angel, and yourself. If an insight is evil, you will most definitely know this because it will excite or stimulate you in some powerful way. An insight truly comes from your angel when it brings with it a sense of peace and quiet rightness. The peace experienced in the depths of the soul will fill you with joy and enthusiasm.

Acceptance

This exercise is very helpful when you are experiencing problems, unhappiness, unfriendliness or obstacles that hinder you from fulfilling your aims and intentions.

On going to sleep, acknowledge the nastiness and misery festering inside.

Look at it dispassionately.

Own it as being a part of you.

Offer it to your angel as a question: *Why am I going through this experience?*

On wakening, acknowledge that you are going through a difficult time.

Accept that this will come to an end.

Say to yourself: *I am willing to bear this burden.*

Accept it as a means to learn more about yourself.

Set out to ask the right questions about what is happening to you, even if they are the questions you most want to avoid asking.

This is a real challenge but nothing is gained easily on the path to insight. Just as cold water refreshes us when we are too hot, so accepting difficulties refreshes the soul. Remember that your angel is always there, and that the obstacle tripping you up at present may actually be the making of your soul.

Seven conditions for esoteric knowledge

Many wise people have said that those who seek insight into the truths of existence must meet certain conditions before they can acquire full knowledge. Here are seven conditions that Rudolf Steiner wrote about in his book called *Knowledge of the Higher Worlds*. (The rendering of these exercises given here comes from personally practising them and having the opportunity to work with them in conjunction with other homemakers.)

One: Strive to live a healthy life.

Two: Be mindful of the fact that everything you do has far-reaching consequences and therefore you and the world are in intimate relationship with each other.

Three: Remember that thoughts have as much effect on others as the blow of a hammer, or the kiss of love.

Four: You can only act from your own centre of existence—that is your real self.

Five: Make a decision, then keep to it (deviate from it only when it is clearly wrong). Then decide on a new, more helpful course of action, and so forth.

Six: Practise gratitude for everything in existence, especially for the things that appear most difficult to be grateful for.

Seven: Make these six practices an integral part of your daily life.

Clearly you don't have to go somewhere private and peaceful to live according to the seven conditions. Rather, you should make them an active ingredient in your daily life. To begin with, however, it is helpful to work for a month on the first, a month on the second, a month on the third, and so on. The best way to do this is to become conscious of how you live in relation to these seven conditions.

Ask yourself questions about each condition, such as: How healthy is my life? How healthy is my food, my sleep, my exercise, etc.? How healthy are my relationships, my thoughts, the books I read, my leisure time? The questions will multiply—which is both stimulating, and sometimes daunting.

Then, of course, come the answers and the obvious need to make your life and the life of others more healthy.

Explore and question all seven in turn, each for a month.
Enjoy the astonishing discoveries.
Try to put them into practice wherever possible.

After that, you can decide yourself which rhythm you use to help you to live by these seven conditions. It is *essential* that you do find a rhythm, be it daily, weekly, monthly, or yearly.

These conditions are a life-long learning curve. The gain comes in developing a consciously constructive lifestyle that supports you in your search for insight and wisdom.

Gratitude

The ground on which the flower of insight grows is the human soul. We are born into a world of suffering and pain, of joy and sorrow, of intentions, actions and reactions. As children, we naturally love the world. It is a vast place to be explored and discovered. We go eagerly into life, or timidly, or fearfully, according to our temperament, upbringing, culture and religion. So much around us shapes our thoughts, feelings and actions.

The whole world is our cradle, school, challenge, joy and, eventually, our grave. There is nothing we meet that does not hold something essential for our karma. That we overlook some things as inessential is our mistake.

Gratitude teaches us not to pass anything by, even if painful, negative or terrifying. It is easy to be grateful for the good, the true and the beautiful. But it is a sobering truth that the pain of life is more formative than the happiness. Contentment, happiness, joy and love of life are certainly things to be grateful for, but the greatest deed of love involves learning to be grateful for *all* that life brings. This is the key that opens the door to deep insight and truth.

8
Finding Freedom

Everyday things that inhibit freedom

Often feeling angry; being bossy; being self-righteous; manipulating situations to suit oneself; putting oneself last; carrying a
hidden agenda; avoiding facing the truth; passing the buck;
tendency to dominate; tendency to be dictatorial; being easily
offended; being eager to please; being bad at taking instructions
or criticism; being stubborn; needing to take charge; keeping
oneself busy; hiding behind a chosen persona; tendency to
personalize issues; feeling the need to defend oneself; inclined to
feeling personally responsible for everything; feeling uncomfortable with sharing; easily feeling threatened; needing respect
for one's position; afraid of being alone; feeling uncomfortable
without background music; avoiding reflecting; feeling dis-
empowered; feeling ineffective.

Reproducing

In love lives the seed of truth
In truth seek the root of love.

These opening lines of a meditation by Rudolf Steiner speak
of love, seeds and truth. We can be lulled into thinking that
our destiny begins at birth and ends at death. This is not so.
Our life between birth and death is a seed in germination.
Death is the chaos a seed undergoes out of which the flower

is born. Life after death is the unfolding and pollinating of the flower, which creates the new seed of a new life on earth. Our next destiny is the germinating seed of the flower of a previous life on earth.

Most people have a sense of purpose, of direction, a sense for where they want to go, where they want to live, which friends they would like to have. Generally, we marry or enter into partnership with someone we choose. For those whose marriages are arranged, either the couple find a common direction recognized by both parties or great unhappiness can result. In most cases, our happiness or unhappiness is the result of our own spiritual choice of destiny, or karma. This truth lies fast asleep inside us. Living meditatively awakens knowledge of karmic truths.

Children who are born to us do not come from nowhere. Many women, and sometimes men too, dream about their unborn child, or have a strong experience of knowing the child and recognizing her at birth, as though welcoming an old friend. Strange as it may seem to people today who are very much in charge of their own life, we do not make our children or choose to have them. They choose us as fit parents for the destiny they are hoping to fulfil. We choose our parents too. While we can never own another person, least of all our children, making friends with them is a great joy.

Certainly, blood ties play a great part in our relationships. But if that were the only or predominant thing, why can one feel like a stranger in one's own family? Or why, having grown up, do we sometimes find little that binds us to family beliefs and customs?

The *life process of reproducing* could also be called the process of truthfully living out our destiny according to our own conscience and by making informed and free choices. It is our potential to create, a deep and powerful spiritual impulse. And yet it can be so difficult to recognize, never mind understand, another's destiny. Often we can only do this with hindsight. Frequently we wish we could have known the outcome of an event before embarking on it, and live sadly with regrets for deeds mistakenly done or left undone.

The process of reproducing in the soul is expressed through the connection between intention, action and consequences. Our inner purpose directs us towards a deed, which makes an imprint upon the world and upon ourselves.

Reproducing in the physical body is expressed in the skills we develop. As soon as we have mastered something we are able to use it for good or evil. We become creator beings through exercising our acquired skills, no matter how insignificant they may seem. Reproducing is active in our reproductive organs, and in our ability to speak. What is said can make or break another person! How delightful it is to observe the development of physical skills in a little child. And how proud they are when a new skill, be it verbal, intellectual or manual, is achieved.

Usually, enjoyment of acquiring new skills goes on all through life. It is the basis of our interests and hobbies, our work and artistic expression. Once we have a certain skill, working, creating, reading or thinking is immensely satisfying. It is also a means of self-expression. What we do often reveals our true nature better than what we say.

We may also want to do things for which we do not yet have the skills. With a sound, strong motive and with hard work and practice we can set out to acquire the capacities we desire. Without a motive to spur us on we might, of course, easily give up.

Motive

It is not always so easy to discern the origin of a motive. Sometimes it arises from our thoughts, or through a feeling, or it can also come from deep within, from an unknown source that pushes us in a certain direction. As the saying goes: *Where there's a will, there's a way.* Extraordinary things can be done once a decision is made and followed through by action.

Motivation is pure force of will, strong and true. It is the inner core of our destiny, of the karma we want to unfold in our present life on earth. It is our true inner sense of purpose. Unfortunately, very few of us have reached the stage of pure loving purpose, thus we also harbour destructive motives. It is therefore helpful to be able to reflect on our motive before embarking on the path our intentions dictate. Our motive may not be quite so pure and true as we wish. A hidden agenda that even we ourselves are not aware of may play in. Drives and desires interweave with motives, colouring destiny, adding to and altering life experiences as we grow and age.

When examining your motive you may occasionally discover that going out to fulfil your intent is essential for your well-being and sense of purpose. You are spurred on by something higher and greater. At such moments you may feel a warm inner glow of angelic empowerment. An awareness of your angel or a power greater than your own soul is at work. You recognize the motive to be connected with your own personal destiny. At such inspired moments there is no fear, hesitation or compromise but only enthusiasm and love for what will come. These moments of enlightenment can become conscious, creative acts of soul if you start to work on acquiring self-knowledge.

Self-knowledge

Most people feel they know themselves very well, better than anyone else does, though in their heart of hearts they might acknowledge this to be a dubious assumption. Secretly, we all know we have a long way to go before we can claim complete self-knowledge. But moments can come in which we surprise ourselves, either for good or ill.

As we go through life we gain life experience, intellectual knowledge and learning, skills of many sorts and also, we hope, self-knowledge. And yet, if asked to be entirely honest, most people will admit to covering up unpalatable truths about themselves.

It is often only when real disaster strikes, when a blow of destiny crushes us, that we can uncover all that lives and weaves inside us, both good and bad. How refreshed we feel when we have looked ourselves straight in the eye, as it were. We may not like what we see but it is a relief to admit faults and failings as well as achievements and purposes, to say with self-knowledge: *This is who I am.*

Examining motivation is a sure road to self-knowledge. This does not mean we should sit down and soul-search before every decision or action. We have reliable everyday skills and knowledge, which we have practised and learned and can use to make our mark in the world without too much forethought. But we are all very familiar with the consequences of taking decisions too lightly, or of not taking decisions at all and just letting events take their course.

We may feel that life passes us by, that we have no say in events, and that as we empower others to fulfil their destiny we are prevented from fulfilling our own. At such times we may manipulate others or lose trust in them, or, worse still, lose trust in our own abilities, skills and self-knowledge.

Homemaking is a personal challenge, preferably undertaken by free choice. If this is not the case, we need to find freedom within the task, to know our motivation and to feel empowered. Every human being has their own value as a striving, developing soul. How this striving is expressed differs from one to another. Recognizing the value of your own inner purpose is the cornerstone of freedom. You need no longer feel trapped. You have become master of your own destiny.

Living with meditation gives a new meaning to life between birth and death. Imaginatively, we might compare meditation to a small foray into life after death. We let go of everyday consciousness and consciously enter the world of the spirit, or the world of higher powers, or the divine creative space. It does not matter what we call it. What matters is that we recognize creator beings, especially the guardian angel. We enable, or empower, ourselves to know with certainty that intention, action and consequence are earthly expressions of life, death and new life, or resurrection.

Meditative exercises for reproducing and motivation

All the exercises so far recommended could, once again, be recommended here. But in strengthening motivation and acquiring spiritual faculties, the actual *practice* of exercises is what enlivens and strengthens the life process of reproducing, of gaining self-knowledge and of discovering your true motive, or purpose for living. There are, however, one or two exercises that specifically assist orientation when searching for your real destiny.

Trust

This exercise is best done in the evening before going to sleep. Find a poem, a thought, a wise saying that encapsulates the above quality. For example: *Light in my thoughts. Peace in my feeling. Love in my deeds.*

Let it fill your mind, heart and soul.
Let it go to your angel.

Some people do this by using a pictorial imagination of their angel. Some people prefer to imagine their angel as a feeling of security and warmth. Some people see their angel as an expression of empowerment. It does not really matter. What matters is that you *trust* in a higher power and that you trust in yourself to be in touch with it.

Empowering

Practise deliberately delegating something to someone else.
Practise believing in their ability to fulfil the task set them.
Practise not interfering unless requested by the other to do so.
Practise informing yourself about how they are getting on *with the sole purpose of offering encouragement.*

Remember to forgive yourself if you get it wrong at first, either by delegating where you should not have done so or by losing trust and reclaiming the task. Just start again. It is immaterial what task you delegate, as long as it is something you always usually do yourself. You will discover that this exercise creates mutual empowerment of the self and the other.

Studying life

Choose five minutes in your day, always at the same time.
Take note of everything that happens in those five minutes.
Before you go to sleep, try to remember every detail.

Or

Take a cut flower in a vase.
Make it an exercise to look at it every day.
Observe how it changes.
Observe it until it has withered away.
Observe its deadness.
Imagine the new life arising from its deadness.

Or

Take a plant, or tree outside.
Practise looking at it every day throughout the year and note the changes.

You will in time begin to be more aware of inner aspects of people, life and events, and how they relate to you and your own purpose in life.

Examining motivation

Choose a specific moment of decision.
Ask yourself why you decided to do it.
Follow up the reason with another: Why?
Continue to ask: Why? Until you know your motive clearly.

It is quite possible that you cannot answer the question at all. Then simply accept that you do not, at this moment, know the reason.

This exercise is best done in the morning, and only once a week, as practised excessively it can lead to self-involvement and self-recrimination, which are extremely counter-productive. Eventually you will want to use this exercise before making a decision of far-reaching importance. This exercise will assuredly lead in time to self-knowledge.

Meditation

Meditating is a very personal thing. If you decide to meditate it will take time out of your day or night. It is, however, time well spent. It is not necessary to meditate for hours. Three minutes will suffice, if this is all the time you can take for it.

It is the quality of silence that refreshes, of putting aside the daily thoughts that waft through your mind, of bringing the body into non-activity, and of devoting your soul to higher beings.

Meditation asks for commitment and repetition. It is best done at the same time every day, and is best kept simple. After some time you may find that the inner peace it formerly gave you fades through familiarity with the meditative content. Feel quite free to choose a new meditation. Familiarity can also, however, go on deepening and broadening the salutary effect.

There are different meditations for different purposes and only you will know which form or content will answer your need. In the busy and often stressful challenges that face us, inner peace and tranquillity is the most reliable and solid basis.

Just as sleep refreshes our whole being, so meditation refreshes and enlivens.

Love

The foundation of life is love, and home is an expression of love. It is natural to human beings to warm to life and other people. We can see this in small children who, if not warned that life is dangerous, have no fear and welcome everything as potentially good. We call this *innocence*. However, as we grow in life experience and knowledge of the world, our fellow men and women hurt, injure, challenge, encourage, love or dislike us. In order to deal with these often abrasive experiences we develop a toughened outer shell behind which we hide our true selves. Thus we are created by others and our environment as much as we create ourselves. We call this *maturity*.

Meditative exercises practised in daily life and meditation itself, for which we need to withdraw from daily life, connect the outer personality with the real self, with self-knowledge, with the self that was born into the world to give and receive love. Thus a new, more aware innocence is born, which we call *wisdom*. Living life wisely and well is the source of peace and freedom.

Epilogue:

A Meditation

Quiet I bear within me
I bear within myself
Forces to make me strong.
Now will I be imbued
With their glowing warmth.
Now will I fill myself
With my own will's resolve.
And I will feel the quiet
Pouring through all my being,
When by my steadfast striving
I become strong
To find within myself
The source of strength,
The strength of inner quiet.

Rudolf Steiner★

★ Rudolf Steiner, *Verses and Meditations* (Rudolf Steiner Press, London)

Bibliography

Books by Rudolf Steiner

Theosophy (Anthroposophic Press, Hudson 1994)

Education for Special Needs (Rudolf Steiner Press, London 1998)

Guidance in Esoteric Training (Rudolf Steiner Press, London 1972)

How to Know Higher Worlds (Anthroposophic Press, London 1994)

Anthroposophy and the Inner Life (Rudolf Steiner Press, Bristol 1994)

Verses and Meditations (Rudolf Steiner Press, London 1972)

Karmic Relationships, Vol. VI (Rudolf Steiner Press, London 1971)

The Gospel of St John (Anthroposophic Press, New York 1962)

The Human Soul in Relation to World Evolution (Anthroposophic Press, New York 1985)

Angels, selected lectures (Rudolf Steiner Press, London 1996)

Sleep and Dreams, selected lectures (SteinerBooks, Great Barrington 2003)

Self Transformation, selected lectures (Rudolf Steiner Press, London 1995)

Evil, selected lectures (Rudolf Steiner Press, London 1997)

Love and its Meaning in the World, selected lectures (Anthroposophic Press, New York 1998)

The Riddle of Humanity (Rudolf Steiner Press, London 1990)

Books by other authors

K. König, *A Living Physiology* (Camphill Books: TWT Publications, Botton 1999)

K. König, *In Need of Special Understanding* (Camphill Press, Botton 1986)

M. Luxford, ed., *The Higher Senses and the Seven Life Processes* (Camphill Books: TWT Publications, Botton 1997)